Second Edition
Skillful 2

Listening & Speaking Teacher's Book

Authors: Emma Pathare and Gary Pathare
Series Consultant: Dorothy E. Zemach

macmillan
education

Macmillan Education
4 Crinan Street
London N1 9XW
A division of Macmillan Publishers Limited

Companies and representatives throughout the world

ISBN 978-1-38000-532-8

Written by Emma Pathare and Gary Pathare

This edition published 2018

First edition entitled "Skillful" published 2012 by Macmillan Publishers Limited

Note to Teachers

Designed by emc design ltd

Cover design by emc design ltd

The publishers would like to thank the following for their thoughtful insights and perceptive comments during the development of the material:

Dalal Al Hitty, University of Bahrain, Bahrain; Karin Heuert Galvão, i-Study Interactive Learning, São Paulo, Brazil; Ohanes Sakris, Australian College of Kuwait, Kuwait; Eoin Jordan, Xi'an Jiaotong-Liverpool University, Suzhou, China; Aaron Rotsinger, Xi'an Jiaotong-Liverpool University, Suzhou, China; Dr. Osman Z. Barnawi, Royal Commission Yanbu Colleges & Institutes, Yanbu, Saudi Arabia; Andrew Lasher, SUNY Korea, Incheon, South Korea; Fatoş Uğur Eskiçırak, Bahçeşehir University, Istanbul, Turkey; Dr. Asmaa Awad, University of Sharjah, Sharjah, United Arab Emirates; Amy Holtby, The Petroleum Institute, Abu Dhabi, United Arab Emirates; Dr. Christina Gitsaki, Zayed University, Dubai, United Arab Emirates.

These materials may contain links for third party websites. We have no control over, and are not responsible for, the contents of such third party websites. Please use care when accessing them.

Printed and bound in Dubai

2022 2021 2020 2019 2018
10 9 8 7 6 5 4 3 2 1

CONTENTS

Map of Student's Book	4
Visual walkthrough	8
Unit 1 Procedural notes	10
Unit 2 Procedural notes	20
Unit 3 Procedural notes	30
Unit 4 Procedural notes	40
Unit 5 Procedural notes	50
Unit 6 Procedural notes	60
Unit 7 Procedural notes	70
Unit 8 Procedural notes	80
Unit 9 Procedural notes	90
Unit 10 Procedural notes	98
Video scripts	108
Answer key	110
Unit assignment marking sheets	123

	Video	Listening	Vocabulary
1 SOCIETY **PAGE 8** **Society** ➤ **Conversation:** Community service **Sociology** ➤ **Lecture:** Can money buy happiness?	A Royal visit	Listen for examples Listen for details	Practice and use verb and noun collocations
2 FOOD **PAGE 26** **Ecology** ➤ **Seminar:** Food waste **Science** ➤ **Lecture:** Brain food	Shelf life	Listen for emphasis of main ideas Predicting	Practice and use phrasal verbs
3 BUSINESS **PAGE 44** **Work** ➤ **Conversation:** Work space **Case study** ➤ **Profile:** Big business	Quiet spaces	Listen for reasons Listen for contrasts	Practice and use business vocabulary
4 TRENDS **PAGE 62** **History** ➤ **Conversation:** Car safety **Geography** ➤ **Lecture:** Urban sprawl	Who's to blame?	Listen for dates Listen for time signals	Practice and use synonyms and antonyms
5 SUCCESS **PAGE 80** **Education** ➤ **Conversation:** Skill: effort or luck? **Society** ➤ **Lecture:** What is success?	Coding school	Listen for vocabulary in context Listen to summarize content	Practice and use prefixes

Grammar	Speaking	Study skills	Unit outcomes
Use discourse markers for adding reasons or details	Notice and practice weak forms Practice giving reasons and explanations Analyze and evaluate which charity to donate to	Managing work and study	Listen for examples to understand evidence in arguments Listen for details in a lecture to follow its organization Discuss, compare, and evaluate two charities
Use relative clauses to add further information	Notice and practice consonant clusters Offer advice and suggestions Present ways to reduce food waste in your local town	Optimal learning to suit you	Practice listening for important information Listen to predict the content of a lecture Evaluate and present suggestions to reduce food waste
Use modal verbs for advice	Chunking a presentation Turn-taking Present a business plan to turn a failing business around	Getting the most out of discussion	Listen to understand a speaker's reasons Distinguish between similar sounds Work with a group to present a business plan
Use the simple past to order historical events	Notice and practice stress patterns in phrases connected with *and* Ask for clarification and repetition Present a timeline of your city	Time management	Listen for dates to understand a timeline Listen for time signals to understand when events happened Describe a timeline of a city's development
Use quantifiers to express approximate quantity	Notice and practice stress in modifiers before data Use discourse markers to compare and contrast Brainstorm, prepare, and present a small talk about passing exams	Studying for tests	Listen to understand key vocabulary in context Listen to summarize what you have heard Compare and contrast data in a presentation about exams

		Video	Listening	Vocabulary
6	**PRESSURE** **PAGE 98** **Sociology** ➤ **Seminar:** Peer pressure **Education** ➤ **Lecture:** Exam pressure	Flower-arranging businessmen	Listen for how opinions are supported Listen for cause and effect	Practice and use collocations with *get*
7	**FEAR** **PAGE 116** **Sociology** ➤ **Seminar:** Fear of public speaking **Social sciences** ➤ **Lecture:** Phobias	Slip sliding away	Listen to recognize organizational phrases Listen to identify problems and solutions	Practice and use the suffixes *-ful* and *-less*
8	**STORIES** **PAGE 134** **Factual story** ➤ **Conversation:** A travel story **English language** ➤ **Lecture:** Elements of a plot	The French Spiderman	Listen to identify the order of events Listen for details to add to a diagram	Practice and use descriptive adjectives
9	**ENVIRONMENT** **PAGE 152** **Technology** ➤ **Seminar:** Solar power **Ecology** ➤ **Presentation:** Eco-tourism	Going green	Listen to recognize pros and cons of an argument Listen to a presenter interact with an audience	Practice and use word families related to the environment
10	**MEDICINE** **PAGE 170** **Technology** ➤ **Seminar:** Face-to-face vs. online doctors **Business** ➤ **Webinar:** Medical tourism	Searching the dirt	Listen to recognize how an argument is supported Listen to determine the speaker's attitude	Practice and use medical vocabulary

Grammar	Speaking	Study skills	Unit outcomes
Use modals in conditional sentences to give advice	Notice and practice consonant sounds at word boundaries Use different techniques to explain something you don't know the word for Brainstorm and discuss ways to reduce academic pressure	Enabling good discussion	Listen to understand how to support an argument Listen to understand cause and effect Analyze, evaluate, and give advice on how to minimize academic pressure
Use the present perfect tense with adverbs to talk about experiences	Notice and practice pausing and pacing speech Use key language to manage questions from the floor Brainstorm, prepare, and present a small talk about a problem you have had to solve	Increasing confidence when speaking	Listen to understand how a speech is organized Listen to identify problems and solutions Deliver a talk on a problem you have had to solve
Use the past progressive to tell a story or experience	Identify, distinguish, and pronounce words beginning with /g/ and /k/ Use words to express your attitude towards something Prepare and tell a factual or fictional story you know	Finding your creative streak	Listen to understand the order of events Listen to select key information to add to a diagram Tell a story
Use modal passives to describe processes and actions	Notice and practice stress with word suffixes Use different techniques to interact with a presenter Present a poster on the environment	Preparing a poster	Listen to identify pros and cons of an argument Listen to understand when and how to interact with a presenter Plan and deliver a poster presentation on the environment
Use indirect questions to be polite	Notice and practice citation, contrastive, and emphatic stress Use different techniques to refute an argument Hold a debate on the impact technology has on patient care	Argument: persuasion through reasons	Listen to understand how an argument is supported Listen to identify the speaker's attitude towards something Prepare for and participate in a debate on technology in medicine

To the teacher

Academic success requires so much more than memorizing facts. It takes skills. This means that a successful student can both learn and think critically. *Skillful* helps teachers prepare their students for academic work in English by teaching not only language—vocabulary and grammar—but the necessary skills to engage with topics, texts, and discourse with classmates.

Teachers using *Skillful* should:

- Encourage students to ask questions and interact. Many of the tasks and exercises involve pairwork, groupwork, and whole-class discussion. Working with others helps students solidify their understanding, and challenge and expand their ability to think critically.

- Personalize the material. Help students make connections between the texts in their book and their own world—home, community, and country. Bring in outside material from local sources when it's relevant, making sure it fits the unit topics and language.

- Provide a lot of practice. Review exercises and material from previous units. Use the *Skillful* digital components to develop the skills presented in the Student's Book.

- Provide many opportunities for review. Remind students of the skills, grammar, and vocabulary they learned in previous units. Have students study a little bit each day, not just before tests.

- Show students how to be independent learners. Point out opportunities to study and practice English outside of class, such as reading for pleasure and using the Internet in English. The Study skills section in every unit gives students valuable tips for successfully managing their own learning.

Learning skills, like learning a language, takes time and practice. Students must be patient with themselves as they put in the necessary time and effort. They should set and check goals. Periodic assessments the teacher can print, such as the unit tests, progress tests, mid and end tests in the digital components let students see their own progress and measure how much they've learned, so they can feel proud of their academic and linguistic development.

Opening page

Each unit starts with two opening pages. These pages get students ready to study the topic of the unit. There is a video to watch and activities to do before class.

Discussion questions

Infographic

Video activities

Unit aims

Opening image

Listening lessons

In every unit, there are two listening lessons and they present two different aspects of the unit topic and help with ideas and language for the speaking task.

Vocabulary to prepare students for the listening activities.

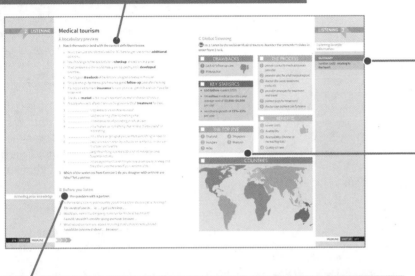

Glossaries help students understand higher-level words from the listening text.

Every listening section helps students use a new listening skill.

Develop your students' listening skills in each stage of the listening lesson.

Speaking lessons

After the listening lessons, there is a page for students to analyze a model answer to a speaking task. This will help organize ideas and language and prepare for the final task at the end of the unit.

Students analyze the model answer.

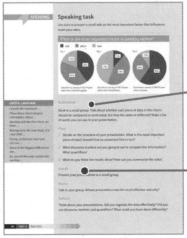

Students brainstorm the speaking task and organize the ideas and language from the unit.

Finally, students perform their speaking task.

Next, they discuss their ideas.

1 SOCIETY

LISTENING 1	Listening for examples
LISTENING 2	Listening for details
STUDY SKILL	Managing work and study
VOCABULARY	Verb and noun collocations
GRAMMAR	Discourse markers for adding reasons or details
SPEAKING	Giving reasons and explanations

Warm-up

If the class is new, start the lesson with a "Getting to know you" activity. Write some facts about yourself on the board (e.g., *name, nationality, number of years as a teacher, favorite food*). Ask students to guess the questions the facts are answers to (e.g., *What's your name? What's your favorite food?*). Tell students to ask you their questions to check. Students then do the same, on paper, with a partner.

Once the class is warmed up, present the aims of the course (to improve listening and speaking skills in an academic context), and look through the course book contents page together, highlighting the structure of units, along with the topics the students will be studying.

Discussion point

Ask students to look at the unit opener image. Elicit different ways people give money to charity (**Possible answers:** *giving money on the street, regular payments from salary, through-TV donations, donating clothes / food / toys*).

Ask students to study the infographic, checking vocabulary as necessary, e.g., *donating*. Then put students into pairs to discuss the three questions. Encourage the students to ask follow-up questions (e.g., *Why do you think that? How can charities support education?*) (**Possible answers:** *individual scholarships, building schools in areas of need*). Elicit the main points of the discussion.

VIDEO

Before you watch

Warm-up

Before starting this section, ask students to brainstorm things they listen to, and / or watch every day in English. On the board, make a list of the things they listen to in English. Ask students to discuss which of these they find easy, or difficult, and if they have any advice or tips on listening that they would like to share with the class.

Highlight the video grab and elicit who is in it (*British Royal Family / Duchess of Cambridge / Kate Middleton*). Elicit any information students may know already about the topic (e.g., *names, ages, background*). Then ask students to discuss and decide if the statements are *T* (True) or *F* (False).

ANSWERS
1 F (They also give food, clothes, advice, and time.)
2 T   3 T   4 F (Prince William also works with charities.)

While you watch

Give students time to read through the questions, before watching the video the whole way through. You can turn on the subtitles if you think your students will benefit from them. Ask students to check in pairs, and then check with the class.

ANSWERS
1 Charities that help young families with children.
2 Volunteers give help to people who need it.
3 It's the center's one-year anniversary of opening.
4 two

See page 108 for the video script.

After you watch

Put the students into pairs, or small groups, and ask them to discuss the questions. Before starting, check the meaning of *do your bit* (**Possible answer**: *make a useful contribution / an effort*). Also, highlight that the questions move from personal opinion (question 1), to experience and knowledge (question 2). When students discuss their answers, encourage them to use follow-up questions, and explore each other's preferences on question 1.

LISTENING 1

Community service

A Vocabulary preview

1 Students work alone to complete the sentences, using dictionaries if they have them. They check in pairs and report back to the class. Elicit from each pair which words they are unable to match (if any), and write these on the board. Ask for feedback from the class to check the answers for these words together, as it is likely that when working together to share whole-class knowledge, most, if not all, of the words will be successfully matched. Students can also complete the *Vocabulary preview* as homework before class.

> **ANSWERS**
> 1 c 2 c 3 a 4 a 5 c 6 a 7 b 8 b

2 Ask students to complete the sentences using the words from Exercise 1. They should then compare their answers in pairs, and then check as a class.

> **ANSWERS**
> 1 fortunate 2 institution 3 donate 4 community service 5 duty 6 consider 7 concept 8 recommendations

B Before you listen

Preparing to listen

As this is the first listening (not including the video) of the book, it is a good idea to raise awareness of the types of texts students will listen to during the course. Elicit the types of situations / listening texts students might listen to in an academic context (**Possible answers:** *lectures, podcasts, tutorials, conversations between students*).

1 Review item 7 from Exercise 1, and item 4 from Exercise 2 in the *Vocabulary preview* section, and highlight that the *Before you listen* section focuses on *community service*. Highlight the *Glossary*, and then give students time to consider the list individually before comparing their ideas in pairs.

2 If possible, ask students to work with a different partner, or to form small groups to share their experiences of community service. Elicit whole-class feedback, asking students to focus on their most valuable experiences.

C Global listening

Listening for main ideas

Give students time to read through the possible main ideas, and check any vocabulary as needed. Play the audio. Ask students to compare their answers in pairs, and then check as a class.

AUDIO SCRIPT

 Track 1.1

PROFESSOR: Hi, Li. What can I do for you?

LI: I need some advice. I'm taking a few classes, but only part-time. I want to use the rest of my time well. Do you have any recommendations?

PROFESSOR: That's a great idea. If it were me, I'd consider doing some community service. It looks very good on your applications for college, graduate school, or employment, so take advantage of it.

LI: What is community service exactly?

PROFESSOR: Basically, it's giving time to help other people who are less fortunate. Usually these people don't have enough money or are in poor health. Service may be for individuals or for institutions.

LI: Institutions? Such as …?

PROFESSOR: Such as schools or hospitals. For example, some volunteers tutor children who need help in their studies in summer school programs. A lot of volunteers work in hospitals. For instance, they donate time to visiting patients who have no relatives or help busy doctors and nurses. I've heard of some volunteers reading to the blind, or working with children with disabilities. There are many other types of volunteering opportunities, too. Sometimes volunteers do manual work like helping build a house or planting trees in a local park. It could also be something very simple, such as giving a ride to people who can't drive. Everyone has a different cause, and it is a good way to make friends.

LI: Hmm, I see. That sounds interesting. Do people do community service mostly to make their applications look good?

PROFESSOR: For some, I think it may start that way. But, in the end, and this is important, overall, I think it's down to not being selfish.

LI: What do you mean?

PROFESSOR: In general, I mean that you should be concerned for others, and take action to help them.

In other words, it is the opposite of thinking of yourself. Many cultures consider caring for the welfare of others as a good characteristic. It's different from feeling that you "need" to do something. You're not simply doing something because you have to. It's not a duty.

LI: I'm not sure I know what you mean.

PROFESSOR: You can show you care about someone by helping them, maybe even someone you don't know, just because you want to. To illustrate, giving up a day to help build a house for a less fortunate family that you may never even meet. It has nothing to do with you, but rather it's all about someone else. Other than feeling good, you, the volunteer, don't benefit; only others benefit. It's been an area of interest for psychologists for many years.

LI: That's interesting. I've been thinking about studying psychology. Maybe this is something to research.

> **ANSWERS**
> ✓ Community service includes volunteering time and service to help others.
> ✓ Volunteers work in different types of public institutions.
> ✓ Caring about others has nothing to do with the person helping, it's about the people receiving the help.

D Close listening

Listening for examples

Highlight that students will be learning a number of listening strategies during the course. Point out that the box contains information about a strategy which the students will then practice. Students can then review these boxes later in the course to make sure they remember, and use the strategies whenever appropriate.

> **ANSWERS**
> Community service – volunteering
> Community institutions – schools, hospitals
> Work at hospitals – visit patients, help doctors and nurses, read to the blind, work with people with disabilities
> Types of manual work – planting trees, building a house

1 Give students time to read through the information, and answer any questions they may have. They should then review the table. They can do this in pairs, recalling any examples they remember from the first listening. Then play the audio again. Students listen and add examples to the table. Go through the answers as a class.

2 Tell students they will listen to excerpts from the discussion, and they should focus on listening for the signal words, or phrases. Go through the answers with the class.

> **ANSWERS**
> 1 For example 2 For instance 3 like 4 such as

AUDIO SCRIPT

🎧 Track 1.2

1 For example, some volunteers tutor children who need help in their studies in summer school programs.

2 A lot of volunteers work in hospitals. For instance, they donate time to visiting patients who have no relatives, or help busy doctors and nurses.

3 Sometimes volunteers do manual work like helping build a house or planting trees in a local park.

4 It could also be something very simple, such as giving a ride to people who can't drive.

E Critical thinking

Supporting critical thinking

Critical thinking is a way of using your experience, observations, research, etc., to justify your own views. It is an essential skill in academic English. Students should not simply accept an argument at face value, but be able to evaluate it, and decide if it is valid, i.e., based on a sound premise. Impress upon students that is it acceptable to have different views, and encourage them to listen to the reasons why others might think differently.

Ask students to read the two questions and consider their answers. Point out that for the second question, students first need to identify their future goals, and then to consider how community service may help achieve them. Also, for each question, students should think of examples to support their views. Then put students into pairs, or small groups to discuss their answers. Encourage debate and exploration of ideas through the use of follow-up questions (e.g., *Why do you say that?*). Ask students to share the main points of the discussions with the whole class.

STUDY SKILLS

Managing work and study

Highlight to students that the *Study Skills* section is a regular part of each unit, and will help them build their study skills as they learn different approaches and techniques.

Ask students, with a show of hands, to indicate whether they work and study, or only study. Then give them time to read through the first part of the box. Then ask students to indicate which of the three categories they are in. Elicit some of the challenges (e.g., *time pressure*). Give time for students to read through the remainder of the box, and then ask them to discuss Exercise 1 in pairs. Encourage students to expand on their answers and think of supporting examples.

Students then rank the benefits in question 2 alone, compare answers with a partner's, and finally discuss the questions in question 3. Ask pairs to report the main points of their discussion to the class.

LISTENING 2

Can money buy happiness?

A Vocabulary preview

1 Students match the words in bold to the definitions. Go through the answers with the class.

```
ANSWERS
1 g  2 d  3 a  4 b  5 c  6 e  7 f  8 h
```

2 Ask students to complete the sentences in pairs, and then check their answers with another pair.

```
ANSWERS
1 experiment  2 cause  3 expensive  4 original
5 provide  6 colleague  7 opposite  8 charity
```

3 Ask students to discuss the questions in pairs. Go through the answers with the class.

B Before you listen

Exam tip

Highlight to students that before listening, it is helpful to consider what you already know, think, or have experienced about a topic. This will activate key ideas and language, which you may then hear in the listening.

1 Students discuss the questions in Exercise 1 in pairs. Elicit feedback from the pairs, and have a Yes / No vote on question 3. Ask students to vote one way or the other, encouraging them to take an overall perspective, and move away from an "it depends" approach. Keep a note of the vote tally; this can be compared to a post-listening vote on the same question.

2 Ask students to recall the meaning of "experiment" (*a test to find out what happens*), and check the meaning of "psychology" with them (i.e., *the study of the mind, and how it affects behavior*). Ask students to complete Exercise 2 in pairs.

```
ANSWERS
2
1 Ask a question about the experiment
2 Describe the experiment
3 Describe the results
4 Answer the question about the experiment
```

C Global listening

Listening for the main ideas

Give students time to read the sentences. Then play the audio. Students compare answers after listening. Also, review the predictions made in Exercise 2 to see if students predicted correctly.

AUDIO SCRIPT

🎧 Track 1.3

Good morning, everyone. Our lecture today will be about charity and happiness. People are taught from a young age that money can't buy happiness, but is that completely true? Maybe giving makes people happier. I'd like to talk about that today and answer this question: Can money make people happy? To answer this question, I will describe some experiments and tell you about the results. Let's find out. Can money buy happiness?

There was an experiment recently where the organizers took a group of college students from the U.S.A. and split them into two groups. They gave both groups an envelope with money in it and asked the first group to spend money on themselves, and tell them how it made them feel. They then asked the second group to be prosocial, which means to use their money to help others, and tell them how that made them feel. Each person in the experiment had different amounts of money. They wanted to see which students would feel happier. All the participants had to do was spend all their money as asked by that evening.

The groups did as they were told and then they had to write down how spending their money that day made them feel. Well, what do you think happened? The students who spent the money on helping other people felt happier than the ones who spent the money on themselves. It didn't matter what amount of money was spent or what it was spent on. Helping others rather than themselves made people happier.

The experiment was also tested in Uganda to see whether there would be any difference. It had the same results! The experiment showed that students buying a cup of coffee for someone made them just as happy as supporting their access to medical care, which is much more expensive. Very different motivation. But the same general results. So doing small things for someone can make you feel just as happy as doing the big things.

The next step was to do a similar experiment in companies. The organizers visited a sales company in New Zealand. Again, they gave some people on the team money to spend on themselves. To other people, they gave them money and asked them to spend it on one of their colleagues. Many of them bought something for the team. Specifically, one team combined their money and bought a piñata and then had fun hitting it together to get the candy. In general, the teams that spent it on their teammates actually performed better in their jobs. In other words, they actually sold more stuff later!

So let's go back to the original question. Can money buy happiness? Well, yes! Even though our parents told us no. When they told us money can't buy happiness, they were wrong. Money can buy happiness ... if you spend it on other people.

That's it for now class. I'll see you next time!

D Close listening

Listening for details

Ask students to study the *Listening for details* box.

Exam skills

Highlight that students should note only the key information when making notes on details, i.e., names, numbers, places, key ideas. This will help them to be able to keep up with the listening. In many exams, the audio is only heard once, so students should try to follow the speaker and not worry if they miss a piece of information.

Play the audio again. As this is the first time students will have listened for detailed information, you could stop the audio after each section, allowing students to compare, and discuss answers with a partner.

POSSIBLE ANSWERS
Question professor wants to answer
    Can money buy happiness?
Describe experiment
    College students in Canada
    Each given an envelope of money
    Half told to spend it on themselves
    Half told to spend it on others
    Also conducted in Uganda
    Also conducted on sales teams at a company
Describe results
    Those that spent money on others were happier.
    It didn't matter how much money it was.
    It didn't matter what the money was spent on—big things, or small things.
Answer the question
    Money can buy happiness ... when you spend it on others.

E Critical thinking

Put students into small groups and ask them to discuss the questions. Highlight the follow-up question *Why / why not?*, and encourage students to use this whenever possible to help each other give extended, justified answers. Again, encourage students to give supporting examples and details when they answer. Elicit feedback from each group. Also, if the class voted earlier, ask students to again vote on whether money can buy happiness. Compare the results and elicit reasons for any changes.

PRONUNCIATION ⟩

Pronunciation for listening
Elision of vowel sounds

As this is the first focus on pronunciation, it may be useful to highlight some of the main areas of pronunciation (stress, intonation, sounds) the students will study, and point out that each unit has a focus on pronunciation for listening, and pronunciation for speaking. Emphasize that the focus of pronunciation for listening is more about understanding rather than producing the target sounds.

Begin this section by clarifying *word stress*. With books closed, write some words from the previous *Vocabulary preview* on the board (e.g., *experiment, charity, provide,* and *cause*). Elicit the number of syllables in each (**Answers:** *4, 3, 2, 1*), and ask which syllable is stressed. Ask students to open their books and read through the information in the box. Say the example words for students. It often helps to give a mispronunciation (e.g., *cho-co-late*) of the word alongside the correct pronunciation, to clarify the sound in focus.

1   Give students time to read the words. Depending how familiar they are with the idea of word stress, students could predict the part of the word they won't hear. Play the audio and have students underline the letters they don't hear. Allow students to compare their answers in pairs before playing the audio again.

AUDIO SCRIPT

🎧 **Track 1.4**

1   every
2   comparable
3   generally
4   different
5   favorite
6   reasonable
7   suppose
8   miserable

ANSWERS

1 every /ˈevri/   2 comparable /ˈkəmp(ə)rəb(ə)l/
3 generally /ˈdʒenrəli/   4 different /ˈdɪfrənt/
5 favorite /ˈfeɪvrɪt/   6 reasonable /ˈriznəbl/
7 suppose /spoʊz/   8 miserable /ˈmɪzrəbəl/

---

2   Ask students to say the sentences to their partner, leaving out the correct letter (a vowel) in the target word. The listening partner should check that the vowel is missed out, and that they understand the word.

Extension activity

Students could dictate the individual words to each other with the correct pronunciation. The listening partner should write down the word, spelling it correctly. When they are finished, give pairs a minute to go through the answers and check they agree. Elicit answers by asking individual listening partners to spell each word out in class.

Vocabulary development
Verb and noun collocations

With books closed, write the verbs *do*, *make*, *give,* and *take* on the board. After *do*, write *homework*. Elicit other nouns from students which go with *do* (e.g., *an exam*, *sport*). Repeat with the other verbs. Ask students to open their books, and give them a minute to read through the box.

1 Students complete the exercise with a partner. Go through the answers with the class.

> ANSWERS
> **1** do **2** give **3** make **4** answer **5** manage
> **6** order **7** take **8** pay

2 Ask students to underline the verb and noun collocations in each question, and then ask and answer the questions with a partner. To finish, ask one or two students each question as a whole class.

Academic words

Highlight to students that they will study words in each unit which are especially important in academic English. Mention there is a special list of words (the Academic Word List) which contains the most important words to know for academic English. The words in this section of each unit are taken from this list.

1 Students read the sentences and match the words in bold with the correct definitions. Encourage students to engage with the sentences containing the words to determine the meaning from context. Tell them to look at the part of speech, and to look for clues about meaning. Ask students to check in pairs, and then check as a class.

> ANSWERS
> **1** h **2** g **3** b **4** a **5** f **6** e **7** d **8** c

2 Ask students to discuss their answers in pairs. For whole-class feedback, ask them to report back the two most interesting question discussions they had.

Speaking model

Give students a minute to read through the information at the start of this section. Highlight that learning is often more effective when we know what we are learning (i.e., *how to give examples, provide reasons,* etc.), and why (i.e., *to present reasons to support a charity of your choice*).

A Analyze

> **Warm-up**
>
> Show the homepage of the website for *Doctors Without Borders*. Ask questions about the page (e.g., *What do you know about this charity? What do you think this charity does?*). Ask students to write four questions they would like answered about the charity. Students can then work in small groups, pooling their questions, and working together to research the answers on the website. Each group can then report their findings to the class.

Ask students to skim-read the *Speaking model* and say how many people are speaking, what the topic is, and whether the speakers agree, or disagree at the end. Then ask the students to read and analyze the model, matching the beginning of the statements with the reasons, or details.

> ANSWERS
> **1** a **2** c **3** b

B Discuss

Students discuss the two questions in pairs, referring closely to the text to find the answers. Go through the answers with the class.

> ANSWERS
> **1** Most of the money actually goes to people.
> **2** I think, In addition, it also

GRAMMAR

Discourse markers for adding reasons or details

As this is the first grammar focus in the book, you could take the opportunity to elicit some of the students' strategies for learning and reviewing grammar (e.g., *using websites*, *keeping an error log*, etc.). Give students the opportunity to explain what they do, and how it helps.

1 Give students a few minutes to study the *Discourse markers for adding reasons or details* box. Then they should work alone to connect the sentences. Monitor and check punctuation. Encourage the students to say the sentences out loud to a partner, pausing appropriately at the comma.

> **POSSIBLE ANSWERS**
> 1 You can volunteer at the hospital because they need people to visit patients. Also, they need people to help the nurses.
> 2 Jana worked for 16 hours without a break and she needs to sleep. Plus, she doesn't want to get sick.
> 3 Peter might do work experience at the hospital because he wants to go to medical school. Furthermore, he wants to help sick people.
> 4 Lily should become president of the volunteer group because she volunteers the most hours. What's more, she knows a lot of charities.
> 5 Kenichi donated all his clothes to the less fortunate. In addition, he donated some money to the food bank in his local community.

2 Students read the situations and add a sentence with another reason. Then put them into pairs and ask each student to say the sentences, again including the correct pausing for punctuation.

SPEAKING

Speaking skill
Giving reasons and explanations

Ask the students to read the information in the *Giving reasons and explanations* box. Focus on the two example sentences and highlight the grammar structure following the phrases (*-ing* form of verb). Then review the sentences, looking at the grammatical context of the sentences. Highlight that although (as is also the case with other sets of linking words and phrases) the linkers share a similar meaning, it is important that they also "fit" grammatically in the sentence.

1 Students work together to complete the sentences with the correct phrase.

> **ANSWERS**
> 1 may be because   2 due to, resulting in
> 3 One consequence of   4 may be due to

2 Put students into small groups. Give them five minutes to discuss the statement. Monitor and encourage students to provide reasons and explanations.

> **POSSIBLE ANSWERS**
> Small charities might give more money to people they help because:
> they have less overhead costs.
> they don't need to pay as many employees.
> they have less to pay on building rent, bills, and administration because there are fewer employees.
> They might not give as much money to people they help because:
> they rely on the money more to pay staff wages.
> they get less financial support than large charities, so more donation money is needed to help run and support the charity.

> **Extension activity**
>
> You could introduce a game element to the discussion by nominating one student as the observer and score-keeper, with one point being awarded for each reason or explanation given. The student with the most points at the end of the discussion is the winner.

PRONUNCIATION

Pronunciation for speaking
Weak forms

Review the work done in the *Pronunciation for listening* section (*Forgotten vowel sounds*), and highlight that in English it is very common for vowel sounds to be reduced, or (as in the previous section) even missed out. With books closed, write a sentence on the board (e.g., *Now we're going to study pronunciation and weak forms*), and elicit which words, or syllables are stressed (*now / go / stu / nun / and / weak / forms*). Then highlight the unstressed words, and elicit what they sound like in the context of the sentence (*we're / to / and*). Point out that these words usually have the *schwa* (ə) sound as the vowel sound. Open books, and give students time to read through the *Weak forms* box.

1 Play the audio, and ask students to circle the number of words in each sentence. After listening to all the sentences, ask students to compare answers, and then listen again to check.

AUDIO SCRIPT

🎧 **Track 1.5**

1 I give money to charity quite often.
2 Some people greet each other by shaking hands.
3 It is customary to bring a present when visiting someone.
4 Our project is based on a children's charity.
5 He regularly volunteers at the elderly home.
6 Everyone should get involved in local community projects.

ANSWERS
1 7 **2** 8 **3** 10 **4** 8 **5** 7 **6** 8

2 Students work in pairs to underline the weak forms in Exercise 2. Check answers in open class.

3 Encourage students to say the sentences out loud to decide, rather than read the sentences in their heads. They should aim at natural pronunciation with rhythm and stress. Students work in pairs, then elicit answers from individual students in class.

ANSWERS
1 I went <u>to</u> <u>the</u> market <u>today</u> <u>to</u> buy ap<u>ples</u>.
2 Daniel wrote <u>an</u> essay <u>about</u> volunteering in <u>his</u> home country.
3 Julie <u>and</u> Nadia <u>are</u> in <u>the</u> same class.
4 My teacher said <u>that</u> I <u>have</u> <u>to</u> study <u>for</u> my test.

SPEAKING

Speaking task
Brainstorm and plan

Before students prepare to present their ideas, ask them to review the content of the unit (vocabulary, grammar, pronunciation), and to identify useful language for the presentation of their ideas. This will help them to achieve the final task more successfully, and also build good study habits of reviewing and applying recent learning.

Explain to the students that they are going to complete a group speaking task. Highlight that they will begin by considering their own views, before sharing these with the group. Point out that this is an effective way to generate the maximum number of ideas, as each group member has the initial time to develop their ideas at their own pace.

Read the task and review the information about the two charities on page 188 as a class. Check any vocabulary as required.

Put the students into groups and assign a charity to each group. Then, working alone, students write a list of reasons to support their charity. Ask the group members to work together and pool their ideas. Set a time limit for the group to choose the three best reasons. Monitor and encourage discussion with reasons and examples.

Then ask groups to rank the reasons they have chosen, and then add supporting ideas for each one. Encourage discussion, with the use of the model language provided. Once all decisions have been made, ask the groups to prepare to present their ideas to another group.

Speak and share

Pair the groups and ask them to present their ideas to each other. Encourage the group acting as the audience to ask questions to explore the reasons further. As the groups present their ideas, take notes on successful and less successful language use, focusing on the language studied in the unit.

Ask each group to work with a new group. They should outline their experience, and the outcome of the presentation of their ideas. Ask the groups to identify ways their presentations could improve to be more persuasive and powerful.

As a whole-class round up, discuss the ways to improve, as identified by the students. Also, provide feedback on the successful and less successful language use you noted, eliciting ways to improve it.

Reflect

Put students into pairs and ask them to discuss the question. Give them three–five minutes. Monitor the discussion, helping with vocabulary where needed.

Wordlist

Students work in pairs or small groups to work through the *Wordlist*, checking that they all remember what each word or phrase means, how to pronounce it, and how it was used in the unit. Go through the list carefully with the class.

Academic words review

Students work through the sentences, check their answers in pairs, and give feedback to the class.

ANSWERS
1 revision **2** principal **3** normal **4** benefit
5 intermediate

Unit review

Students work through the list alone to decide what they can and can't do. They discuss their answers in pairs, including what they remember from the unit about each point. Finally, open up the discussion to include the whole class. Pay particular attention to any boxes that the students didn't check. Explore with them ways of overcoming any remaining problems.

Extra research task

As a take-home activity, ask students to research a charity which supports a cause they care about. Students can share the information they find with the class in the following lesson.

LISTENING 1	Listening for emphasis of main ideas
LISTENING 2	Predicting
STUDY SKILL	Optimal learning
VOCABULARY	Phrasal verbs
GRAMMAR	Relative clauses
SPEAKING	Offering advice and suggestions

Warm-up

Write *Food* in the center of the board, and then build a mind map with *Fruit and vegetables, Meat, Cereals, Dairy,* and *Fish* at the end of branches coming off the central word. Elicit an example of each category (**Possible answers:** *apple, chicken, bread, milk, tuna*), and then ask students to work in pairs to brainstorm more items in each category. Students come to the board to write up their words.

Discussion point

Ask students to look at the unit opener image. Ask what global problem the image shows (**Answer:** *food waste*), and elicit how much students know about the topic. Ask if they consider food waste a problem globally, and also in their own country.

Ask students to study the infographic and discuss the questions with a partner. Ask for feedback on the reasons individuals, restaurants, and supermarkets waste food. Draw three columns on the board, one for each category, and add students' ideas to each one. Highlight any reasons which are in more than one category. Add a fourth column with the heading *Solutions,* and add the students' ideas.

VIDEO

Before you watch

1 Read through the information about the video the students are going to watch. Then ask the students to discuss the bold words, checking the meaning of the words in a dictionary as necessary. Highlight that the verbs in questions 4 and 5 are phrases, and that students need to check the meaning of these carefully in the dictionary.

ANSWERS
1 1 Food is wasted when it is not eaten; too much food is produced; it goes off / out of date.
 2 **Possible answers:** Some food which is out of date is still OK to eat, stores put a date that is "best eaten before," but doesn't mean it's bad to eat it; it might make you sick if you eat food that has gone bad / gone off.
 3 Moldy: fruit, bread (if stored in plastic), cheese; Stale (if left in the open air): cookies, bread, cake
 4 If it's out of date; if food is left out of a fridge / stored badly; oxygen reaches the food and makes it moldy / stale.
 5 Students' own answers

2 Put students into pairs, and ask students to take turns asking and answering the questions. Monitor the activity to help with vocabulary where necessary.

3 Read through the list of items in *Before you watch,* Exercise 3, checking the meaning as necessary. Then give students time to discuss the items, and the possible science experiment with their partner. Remind them that the experiment is to do with keeping food fresh, and encourage the students to speculate as to what this experiment might involve.

While you watch

Go through the answers as a class.

ANSWERS
plastic, bread, crab shells, bottles, mold
POSSIBLE ANSWER
These things are all part of an experiment in the video which researches environmentally friendly plastic.

See page 108 for the video script.

After you watch

Put students into pairs and set a time limit for students to discuss the questions. After they have talked about each question, put pairs together to form small groups, and ask the students to explain their ideas to each other. Ask for feedback on question 3 (*Should governments spend money researching new types of food packaging?*) as a whole class, and write the *Why / why not?* (for and against) ideas on the board. Ask for an overall vote on the issue when all the ideas have been written up.

ANSWERS

1 Normal *polyethylene* plastic makes bread go moldy after a few days; an environmental impact is also plastic pollution. (According to Harvard University's Wyss Institute, humans produce 300 million tons of plastic per year … the remaining 97% is dumped in landfills and oceans, harming the food chain, and the environment.)

2 It doesn't contain bad chemicals for your body (**Alternative possible answer:** it is biodegradable, and better for the environment).

LISTENING 1 >

Food waste

A Vocabulary preview

1 Write the bold words on the board, and ask students which ones they know. Elicit the meaning of each known word from around the class. Indicate if the meaning given by students is incorrect, but avoid clarifying the correct answers, or writing up any of the suggestions. Ask students to guess at the words they don't know. Students then open their books and match the words to the definitions. Go through the answers with the class. Check the pronunciation of each word, particularly the multi-syllable words (*solution, agriculture*), and the two-syllable words (*profit, hunger, billion, challenge*).

ANSWERS

1 g 2 d 3 a 4 e 5 c 6 h 7 f 8 b

---

2 Students work alone to complete the sentences with the words in bold from Exercise 1. Ask students to check in pairs, and then check as a class.

ANSWERS

1 challenge 2 hunger 3 feed 4 waste
5 agriculture 6 billion 7 profit 8 solution

B Before you listen
Activating prior knowledge

Exam tip

Ask students to identify which of the questions is asking about personal experience (**Answer:** *question 1*), and which ask about more general, abstract ideas (**Answer:** *questions 2 and 3*). Highlight that in many exams, candidates are expected to be able to discuss both question types, usually starting on the personal level (e.g., IELTS Speaking Parts 1 and 2), and then moving to the more abstract (IELTS Speaking Test Part 3). Elicit the type of verb tenses likely to be found in the different types of questions (**Possible answer:** *personal—concrete tenses, e.g., simple present / past / progressive, present / past perfect; abstract— conditional, e.g., would, could, etc.*).

Students work in pairs or small groups to discuss the questions. During whole-class feedback, ask students to report back only the biggest problem (question 2), and the simplest solution (question 3). Discuss any disagreements that arise.

C Global listening
Listening for emphasis of main ideas

Warm-up

With books closed, write the following sentence on the board: *Emphasis helps you understand and remember important information.* Underline *important* and elicit what the underlining does (**Possible answer:** *emphasizes the word*). Elicit and suggest other ways of emphasizing in writing (**Possible answers:** *use an exclamation point, write in capitals, circle words, write words in bold, use particular words and phrases*), and apply some of these to the key words in the sentence. Then elicit ways we emphasize ideas when we speak (**Possible answers:** *speaking loudly, pausing, using particular words and phrases, repetition*).

Give students time to read through the *Listening for emphasis of main ideas* box. Highlight the use of the word *signal,* and explain how listeners use signals to predict and understand the organization of the coming speech.

Students read through the four sentences to be completed before listening, and writing the missing words. Ask students to check the spelling of the phrases with the phrases in the skills box.

AUDIO SCRIPT

🎧 Track 2.1

JULIA: Why didn't you get an apple with your lunch today, Sofia? You always get an apple.

SOFIA: Well, after hearing Dr. Cray's lecture today, I was thinking about the apples I buy every day. I usually eat half and then throw the rest out. Now that I know more about it, I am going to eat fewer apples.

JULIA: I know what you mean. I waste stuff all the time. What about you, Amira?

AMIRA: Me, too. I'm going to be a lot more careful when I choose things from the buffet in the future. I feel like we need to do something. But, it's not going to really solve the problem on a global scale. What do you think, Julia?

JULIA: I'm worried about the amount of food that some supermarkets waste. I can't believe they throw out fruit and vegetables that are imperfect … you know … that have some bad qualities. In other words, just because it looks bad, they throw it out rather than use it.

SOFIA: It's important to note that not all supermarkets are bad. I liked the part of the lecture when Dr. Cray talked about some supermarkets having an "ugly" food section—like where they put all the bad-looking fruit. I would buy from that section.

AMIRA: Well, what really annoyed me was the fact that some supermarkets focus too much on money. I understand that fresh fruit and vegetables result in 15% of their profits, but what is more important? Profit or the environment?

JULIA: In general, I think we need to focus on a bigger problem: the environment. Dr. Cray said that the amount of food waste from stores and consumers, the people who shop at those stores, equaled a loss of 133 billion dollars!

SOFIA: It just shocked me that food waste is the largest part of the trash in landfill sites—larger even than paper or other household trash. We just throw it all in an enormous hole in the ground—such a waste. And the real problem with that? The wasted food turns into methane, which is bad for the environment.

AMIRA: Yeah, didn't he actually say that landfills are the third largest source of methane in the United States?

SOFIA: Yeah, he did. But, what I didn't know was how damaging methane is. I knew it was a greenhouse gas. Overall, it stops the heat from escaping from the atmosphere and causes the greenhouse effect, which causes global warming, but I didn't know it was more damaging than carbon dioxide.

JULIA: I can't believe that we waste about 1.6 billion tons of food per year. That could cover the city of Madrid in Spain! Which makes me think that damaging the environment is not the only problem caused by wasted food. What about world hunger?

AMIRA: You're right. That's next week's lecture. It's on world hunger, so we should definitely attend it now because that's also linked to food waste and global warming.

ANSWERS

1 In other words,   **2** It's important to note that
3 In general,   **4** Overall,

D Close listening

Listening for additional information

1 Give students time to read through the questions. Then play the first part of *Food waste* again, and ask students to match the names. Go through the answers with the class.

AUDIO SCRIPT

🎧 Track 2.2

JULIA: Why didn't you get an apple with your lunch today, Sofia? You always get an apple.

SOFIA: Well, after hearing Dr. Cray's lecture today, I was thinking about the apples I buy every day. I usually eat half and then throw the rest out. Now that I know more about it, I am going to eat fewer apples.

JULIA: I know what you mean. I waste stuff all the time. What about you, Amira?

AMIRA: Me, too. I'm going to be a lot more careful when I choose things from the buffet in the future. I feel like we need to do something. But, it's not going to really solve the problem on a global scale. What do you think, Julia?

JULIA: I'm worried about the amount of food that some supermarkets waste. I can't believe they throw out fruit and vegetables that are imperfect … you know … that have some bad qualities. In other words, just because it looks bad, they throw it out rather than use it.

ANSWERS

1 Sofia   **2** Amira   **3** Julia

---

2 Students read through the items and options for answers before listening to the next part. Before listening, focus on the answers which are similar sounding (i.e., questions 1 and 2), and ask students to read the different options out loud to themselves, to raise awareness of what they will be listening for. After listening, give students time to check in pairs. Play the audio again if appropriate, stopping after each answer to check together as a whole class.

AUDIO SCRIPT

🎧 Track 2.3

SOFIA: It's important to note that not all supermarkets are bad. I liked the part of the lecture when Dr. Cray talked about some supermarkets having an "ugly" food section—like where they put all the bad-looking fruit. I would buy from that section.

AMIRA: Well, what really annoyed me was the fact that some supermarkets focus too much on money. I understand that fresh fruit and vegetables result in 15% of their profits, but what is more important? Profit or the environment?

JULIA: In general, I think we need to focus on a bigger problem: the environment. Dr. Cray said that the amount of food waste from stores and consumers, the people who shop at those stores, equaled a loss of 133 billion dollars!

SOFIA: It just shocked me that food waste is the largest part of the trash in landfill sites—larger even than paper or other household trash. We just throw it all in an enormous hole in the ground—such a waste. And the real problem with that? The wasted food turns into methane, which is bad for the environment.

AMIRA: Yeah, didn't he actually say that landfills are the third largest source of methane in the United States?

SOFIA: Yeah, he did. But, what I didn't know was how damaging methane is. I knew it was a greenhouse gas. Overall, it stops the heat from escaping from the atmosphere and causes the greenhouse effect, which causes global warming, but I didn't know it was more damaging than carbon dioxide.

JULIA: I can't believe that we waste about 1.6 billion tons of food per year. That could cover the city of Madrid in Spain! Which makes me think that damaging the environment is not the only problem caused by wasted food. What about world hunger?

AMIRA: You're right. That's next week's lecture. It's on world hunger, so we should definitely attend it now because that's also linked to food waste and global warming.

ANSWERS
1 B **2** C **3** B **4** A **5** A

E Critical thinking

Ask students to read through the questions on their own and a make a note of their answers. They then work in small groups to discuss the questions. Highlight that critical thinking goes beyond identifying (e.g., *What types of food do you usually throw away?*) to focus more on analyzing (e.g., *Why?*). Encourage students to answer the question *Why?* in relation to question 2, too. Highlight that the critical thinking skill in question 3 involves finding creative solutions. Ask each group to report back on the main points of discussion.

STUDY SKILLS >

Optimal learning to suit you

With books closed, ask students for ideas about how to do the best they can in their own particular learning context. Elicit key factors (**Possible answers:** *technology, time, course, materials, classes*). Elicit ideas on how they can use these factors to make sure they are learning in the best way they possibly can. Students then open books and read through the box. Ask them to identify words they are not sure of, and check the meaning in dictionaries if they have them (e.g., *relevant, combination / combine, pace*). Point out the *Glossary*, and check students' understanding of these words.

1   Ask students to read through the questions alone and make a note of their answers. They then compare their answers with a partner's. Elicit feedback from student pairs, asking them to report on any major differences between the answers. Highlight that there is no right or wrong answer. The issue is one of personal preference, as long as students are confident their choices are working for them, and can find evidence for this (e.g., good results).

2   Students complete the sentences alone, and then compare their ideas with a partner's.

Brain food

A Vocabulary preview

1 Ask students to work alone to read the sentences and choose the best definition. They then compare their answers with a partner's, and use a dictionary for a final check if necessary.

> **ANSWERS**
> **1** a **2** a **3** a **4** a **5** b **6** b **7** a **8** b

2 Students work in pairs to discuss which statements they agree with. Encourage them to support their opinions with evidence, whether personal, or from research they have read. Ask students to share the main points of disagreement with the class. Open these points up to a whole-class discussion.

B Before you listen

Activating prior knowledge

> **Warm-up**
>
> Write different parts of the body on the board, e.g., *bones*, *skin*, *hair*, *blood*, *heart*, *muscles* (but not *brain*). Then write *milk,* and draw a line to *bones*. Elicit the connection (**Answer:** *Milk is good for bones because it contains calcium which makes bones stronger.*). Ask students to discuss other connections between food and the health of different parts of the body. Work as a whole class to share ideas, and build up the information on the board. (**Possible answers:** *bones—yoghurt, cheese; skin—fruit and vegetables, not sugar; hair—olive oil; blood—red meat, green vegetables; muscles—protein*).

Ask students to discuss the questions in pairs, and then check as a class. Identify any parallels between taking care of the body and the mind (e.g., *how do students rest their bodies?—by lying / sitting down, and how do they rest their minds?—by relaxing in a quiet place, sleeping, doing something they enjoy*).

C Global listening

Predicting

Give the students time to read through the *Predicting* box. Check the meaning of key words (e.g., *anticipate*, *develop*, *strategies*, *notice*).

> **Extension activity**
>
> Ask students to study the *Predicting* box for a minute. They then close their books, and recall the approach to take to predicting before listening. Build up the information from the box on the board. When finished, ask students to open their books and compare the information in the box with the information they recalled as a class. (This is a useful strategy for encouraging students to engage with the skills boxes, which can be used at any point during the course.)

1 Students discuss the questions with a partner. Emphasize that at this point, there is no right or wrong answer. Students are predicting or making "an educated guess," drawing on their world knowledge, and prior knowledge of the topic.

2 Explain to students they are going to listen to the radio interview to check which of their predictions were correct. Ask students to discuss their answers in pairs, and then check as a class.

AUDIO SCRIPT

 Track 2.4

HOST: Good morning everyone. Today we're talking to Dr. Nathan Williams. Dr. Williams is a food expert who is going to talk about a different way to stay healthy: mentally healthy. Welcome Dr. Williams.

DR. WILLIAMS: Thanks for having me.

HOST: So, what is brain food?

DR. WILLIAMS: It is food that is believed to be good for the brain. I know a lot of your listeners are students who might like coffee in the morning or look forward to snacking on chocolate candy in the afternoon. Well, coffee contains caffeine, which is a substance that makes us more active. Caffeine can be considered a brain food because it helps you wake up. Researchers have also found out that caffeine can help to improve your concentration. Chocolate contains sugar and can help you to focus. Although we hear a lot about the bad effects of sugar, something sugary might improve your memory. Like all foods, however, it's temporary and the effects of caffeine and sugar decrease over time.

HOST: If our brains react to sugar and chocolate, and it helps us pay attention, do you suggest we all eat more?

DR. WILLIAMS: Well, the kind of sugar that the brain really wants isn't regular sugar. It's really the type of sugar that comes after we eat foods like bread. It's a sugar that the body makes from certain foods. A good source is fruit, and sadly not chocolate. If it were me, I'd avoid too much chocolate because the temporary good effects aren't worth the permanent bad effects on the body.

HOST: Well, I'm sad. I have to give up chocolate.

DR. WILLIAMS: Well, it's fine to eat chocolate occasionally. I would recommend dark chocolate—it's known to be healthier than milk chocolate. If I were you, I'd choose a dark chocolate with nuts, like peanuts, or almonds. Just a small amount of chocolate and nuts gives your brain food to keep it going.

HOST: Great. Now, moving on from chocolate, I've always heard that fish is a brain food. Is it?

DR. WILLIAMS: It is. And this is a food that has a more positive impact because it has effects that last longer. Fish provides protein and other good things that feed the brain. It is also good for your heart, so your body and your mind feel great.

HOST: That's interesting. I often eat fish for dinner. I'm wondering when is the best time to eat brain food? Is dinner a good time?

DR. WILLIAMS: Actually, I recommend mornings. I think the key is having a good breakfast when you wake up. It's important to eat well after a long sleep. I would suggest including cereal, milk, and fruits, which are good brain foods. You can remember more and remember it for a longer time after a healthy breakfast. A popular breakfast fruit like blueberries can improve how much you learn. And on the subject of breakfast, I'd like to point out that cereals aren't just good for your mental health. According to statistics, they're also good for your physical health.

HOST: The idea of brain foods is certainly becoming more popular, but Dr. Williams, is there any evidence that brain foods can make you smarter?

DR. WILLIAMS: There is always some debate about whether or not these foods really do make you smarter, but if you ask me, no food, or drink can really raise your IQ. Intelligence depends on many factors, and eating good food is just one way of helping your brain work to its potential. So, brain foods on their own won't make you a more intelligent person, but feeding your brain can help in other ways.

HOST: So what would your advice be to our listeners who want to improve their brain nourishment?

DR. WILLIAMS: I'd recommend eating fewer of the negative foods and adding more positive brain foods into your diet.

HOST: Thank you for the food for thought, Dr. Williams. You've given us a lot to think about.

ANSWERS
1 Because they are "good" for the brain.
2 dark chocolate, fish, coffee, cereal, milk, blueberries
3 They can improve how much you learn, your mental health, and your physical health.

D Close listening

Listening for details

1 Read through the list of food and drink with students, and check meaning and pronunciation, particularly of the word stress in *chocolate*, *strawberries*, and *vegetables*. Students read the three benefits and predict which food they pair with. They then listen to sections of the interview, and check.

AUDIO SCRIPT

🎧 **Track 2.5**

1 **DR. WILLIAMS:** Chocolate contains sugar and can help you to focus. Although we hear a lot about the bad effects of sugar, something sugary might improve your memory. Like all foods, however, it's temporary, and the effects of caffeine and sugar decrease over time.

2 **DR. WILLIAMS:** A popular breakfast fruit like blueberries can improve how much you learn. And on the subject of breakfast, I'd like to point out that cereals aren't just good for your mental health. According to statistics, they're also good for your physical health.

3 **HOST:** Great. Now, moving on from chocolate, I've always heard that fish is a brain food. Is it?

DR. WILLIAMS: It is. And this is a food that has a more positive impact because it has effects that last longer. Fish provides protein and other good things that feed the brain. It is also good for your heart, so your body and your mind feel great.

ANSWERS
1 c 2 a 3 b

---

2 Give students time to read through the sentences and discuss them with a partner. Again, they could predict the answers at this point, before listening to the complete interview to check. When checking answers as a whole class, elicit student views. Ask: *Which information did you know already? Which information surprises you? Which do you have personal experience with?* Encourage the students to share their views with the other students.

ANSWERS
1 similar   2 memory   3 short   4 chocolate
5 dark   6 breakfast   7 cannot

E Critical thinking

Students work in small groups to discuss these questions. Ask students to report the main views that arose from question 3 to the class. Encourage them to consider both the positive and negative impact of food.

Extension activity

On the board write *Compare*, *Assess*, and *Identify*. Ask students to review the questions in the *Critical thinking* section, and match the words to the question functions. (**Answer:** *question 1—identify; question 2—compare; question 3—assess*). Highlight to students that, as well as practicing critical thinking skills, it is also useful to identify which actual skills are being used.

PRONUNCIATION >

Pronunciation for listening
Stress in phrasal verbs

Warm-up

With books closed, write *go bad* and *throw away* on the board. Remind students these verbs were in the video about food waste. Ask them what the verbs mean, and if they remember what the name of this type of verb is (**Answer:** *phrasal verb*). Students then open their books, and read the information in the box. Ask students to listen to you saying the three verbs from the box, and the two on the board. Say them with both correct stress and incorrect stress (i.e., stressing the verb and not the particle and vice-versa), and ask students to identify which is correct.

1   Give students time to read through the sentences. They could predict which particle is missing at this stage. Students then listen, check, and note the missing word. Students check their answers in pairs. Play the audio again as necessary.

AUDIO SCRIPT

🎧 **Track 2.6**

1   I'd like to point out that cereals aren't just good for your mental health.
2   I know a lot of your listeners look forward to snacking on chocolate candy in the afternoon.
3   Researchers have also found out that caffeine can help to improve your concentration.
4   Now, moving on from chocolate, I've always heard that fish is a brain food.
5   Caffeine can be considered a brain food because it helps you wake up.

6   I can't believe they throw out fruit and vegetables that are imperfect.
7   I was thinking about the apples I buy every day.

ANSWERS

1   out   2   to   3   out   4   on   5   up   6   out   7   about

2   On the board, write *make up* and *approve of*. Elicit the difference in the form of the two main verbs, i.e., that *make* has one syllable, and *approve* has two. Ask which syllable in *approve* is stressed (**Answer:** *the second*). Students then identify the phrasal verbs in the sentences in their books. They should then identify if the main verb has one, or more than one syllable. If it has more than one, they then need to identify which one is stressed. Students then listen and check. They can compare answers in pairs, and listen again to check if necessary.

AUDIO SCRIPT

🎧 **Track 2.7**

1   The instructor moved on from the small talk and focused on the lecture about wasted food.
2   The substitute is going to take over while the instructor is away at a conference on food waste.
3   Juan Pablo never runs away from a challenge and he is going to find a solution for all the food waste in the cafeteria.
4   Angelina tried to get ahead of the food waste problem by looking for a solution before the university declared it an issue.

ANSWERS

1   moved on from /muvd ɑn frɑm/   2   take over /teɪk ˈoʊvər/   3   runs away from /rʌnz əˈweɪ frɑm/   4   get ahead of /gɛt əˈhɛd əv/

VOCABULARY >

Vocabulary development
Phrasal verbs

Warm-up

Mime some actions for the students, in order to elicit some common phrasal verbs, and write these on the board. (**Possible answers:** *get up* [e.g., from sitting], *turn off / on* [the light], *look up* [a word in the dictionary]). Knowing they are already familiar with some phrasal verbs should help to build students' confidence regarding this area of language, before studying them more in depth.

1 Give students time to read through the *Phrasal verbs* box. Highlight to students that when learning phrasal verbs, it is useful to learn them as "chunks" of language, using sample sentences to see how the particular phrasal verbs function (some students can find the technical rules off-putting.) Students then work alone to match the phrasal verbs with their synonyms. Allow time for students to check their answers in pairs.

> **ANSWERS**
> **1** e **2** f **3** d **4** c **5** b **6** a

2 Students then work alone to complete the questions with a phrasal verb from Exercise 1. Check answers as a class.

> **ANSWERS**
> **1** get up **2** give up **3** turn into **4** point out
> **5** throw out **6** find out

3 Students discuss the questions in pairs. Ask them to report back on the question for which their answers were most similar answer, and the question for which their answers were most different.

VOCABULARY 〉

Academic words

1 Ask students to complete the exercise alone, then check in pairs, and then check as a class. Review the pronunciation of the words, particularly the word stress of the multi-syllable words (*strategy, evidence, statistics, physical, participate*).

> **ANSWERS**
> **1** d **2** c **3** e **4** a **5** h **6** f **7** g **8** b

2 Students discuss the questions in pairs. After a few minutes, put pairs together to form small groups, and encourage students to share the main points of their discussions. Elicit whole-class feedback on questions 1, 4, and 5. Collect ideas on the board, and a class vote can be conducted for each question (i.e., *mental health* vs. *physical health*; *the most important benefit*; *the best strategy*).

SPEAKING 〉

Speaking model

Extra support: Read through the overview of the *Speaking* section with the students. Ask them to identify the speaking skill, the grammar, and the pronunciation focus (**Answers:** *giving advice, defining relative clauses, consonant clusters*). Remind the students that this information shows how everything they do in the *Speaking* section builds towards the final task.

A Analyze

Give students time to read and complete the speaking model. After checking the answers, ask the students what is the overall problem talked about, and where (**Answers:** *litter; Kimperley*). Ask what evidence the speaker has about this problem (**Answer:** *statistics, and personal experience*).

> **ANSWERS**
> **1** there are over 100,000 inhabitants **2** the things they don't want **3** providing more waste bins **4** to clean up the streets

B Discuss

Students work in pairs or small groups to discuss the questions. Monitor and encourage students to expand on their answers to each question. For question 1, they should provide evidence and examples; for question 2, students should justify their answers; and for question 3, they should think creatively to come up with more solutions. Monitor the activity and help with vocabulary where needed.

GRAMMAR 〉

Relative clauses

Give students some time to read through the *Relative clauses* box. Write two sentences from the box on the board: *There's someone in my class whose parents are famous* and *England is the country where I'd most like to visit.* Then ask students to tell you what they have learned about relative clauses, using these two sentences to prompt the students. Elicit the other relative pronouns used (**Answer:** *who, which, that, when*), and what the extra information does (**Answer:** *gives more detail, and defines the noun in the main part of the sentence*). Elicit the difference between the first and second sentence (**Answer:** *whose cannot be deleted from the sentence, but where can.*). Explain that the reason for this is because relative pronouns that refer to the object of a sentence can be removed. (**Answer:** *It refers to the object of the sentence.*). Ask students to recall what commas around the relative clause show (**Answer:** *That the information is not essential, and can be removed.*).

1. Students work alone to underline the relative clauses. They can check their answers in pairs.

2. Students decide if the relative pronouns can be removed. Go through the answers to both questions 1 and 2 as a class.

> **ANSWERS**
>
> **1 and 2**
>
> 1. The last time we saw each other was <u>when we were in Mrs. Kingston's class</u>.
> 2. The store <u>where I usually buy my stationery</u> is closed.
> 3. The man, <u>whose job it is to fix the computers,</u> hasn't finished.
> 4. The students, <u>whose grades were low</u>, had to retake the test.
> 5. Two thousand sixteen was <u>when I graduated school</u>.
> 6. I remember the day <u>when I got my exam grades</u>. I was very nervous. [Relative pronoun can be removed.]

3. Students work in pairs to combine the sentences using relative clauses. Go through the answers with the class.

> **ANSWERS**
>
> 1. The woman, whose job it is to order books, is a library assistant.
> 2. Eduardo, whose exam is tomorrow, is studying.
> 3. Last week, when we did the experiment, it failed.
> 4. Spain, where it can get very hot in the summer, is a popular tourist destination.

SPEAKING ▷

Speaking skill
Offering advice and suggestions

> **Warm-up**
>
> With books closed, tell students that you have a problem and need some advice. Say you are having difficulty concentrating on work today. Ask for their suggestions. Write the key words from each suggestion on the board (e.g., *eat chocolate, take a short nap*). After students read through the information in the *Offering advice and suggestions* box, ask them to reformulate the ideas into suggestions with correct grammar.

1. After reading through the skills box, students work alone to correct the mistakes. Give them time to check in pairs and then check as a class.

> **ANSWERS**
>
> 1. One idea is donating more food to charities.
> 2. I'd recommend avoiding eating too much food in the evening.
> 3. How about buying imperfect fruit at the market?
> 4. It might be a good idea to save food from ending up in the landfills.
> 5. I suggest using leftover food for compost or to feed farm animals.
> 6. You should buy food from the "ugly" section of the market.

2. Students work in pairs to complete the dialogues. Encourage them to focus on ideas first, and then the accuracy of the grammar when they write the sentences. Note questions 1, 2, and 4 need the *-ing* form. Monitor and check answers as the students work. Then ask them to practice the dialogues, building up to doing them from memory, rather than reading them off the page.

3. Students work in small groups and take turns asking for advice, based on the three situations given. Monitor and make a note of language used, both effective examples, and language which can be improved.

> **Extension activity**
>
> Write up examples of effective language use, and sentences to be corrected from the group discussions in Exercise 3. Work together as a whole class to identify correct examples, and to improve the incorrect examples.

4. Elicit examples of advice for each situation from the different groups, and for each one, encourage the class to evaluate how useful the advice is.

PRONUNCIATION ▷

Pronunciation for speaking
Consonant clusters

Read through the *Consonant clusters* box with the students. You could point out to students that many languages have far fewer consonant clusters than English, and this can cause problems for learners of English. A common strategy that learners (wrongly) employ is to insert vowel sounds between the consonants to break up the clusters. When modeling the words in the box for the students, use exaggerated facial movements to highlight where in the mouth each sound is made, and then gradually say the word with more speed, bringing the two sounds together; for example, *blue*: *b* (lips), *l* (tongue and top of mouth).

1   Students listen to the words, and underline those they hear. Then they listen again and repeat.

AUDIO SCRIPT

🎧 **Track 2.8**

1 clue
2 braise
3 flame
4 fly
5 free from
6 green glasses
7 clean room
8 brew tea

ANSWERS
1 clue   2 braise   3 flame   4 fly   5 free from
6 green glasses   7 clean room   8 brew tea

2   Students work in pairs, identifying the words in Exercise 1 their partner says.

3   Read through the example sentence with students, and ask them to practice saying it. Then monitor while students write and practice their own sentences. Encourage the students to use as many consonant blends as they can. (The language should be accurate, but students don't need to worry about how sensible the sentence is.)

4   Students discuss the questions. Monitor and refocus students on the correct pronunciation of the consonant clusters as necessary.

SPEAKING ▷

Speaking task
Brainstorm and plan

Open books and read the task together. Check any vocabulary as required. Students work alone to rank the strategies for reducing wasted food. When they have completed the ranking, put students into pairs, and ask them to compare their views and explain them. Then together they should think of two more possible strategies.

Students work alone again to select three ideas in total; two from the list, and one from the ideas the pairs produced together. Students then make notes on their own advice and suggestions, based on these ideas, for the local government planning committee. Students should make a note of examples and evidence to support their advice and suggestions.

Speak and share

Students work with a new partner to present their advice and suggestions. Monitor and take note of language use related to the unit for whole-class feedback later.

Students then change partners, and report on the advice and suggestions they just heard. Ask students to identify the best advice their partner gave, the best advice they feel they gave, and say if they would change anything the next time they talked on the same topic.

Reflect

Students reflect on the question, and discuss how they can have an impact on food waste where they live. Encourage students to consider the individual level, e.g., *in the home*, and also on a *community level*.

Extension activity

Ask students to keep a journal for a week focusing on food waste they see happening. *What examples of food waste do they notice? What actions do they take to prevent it? What actions do they see other people taking?* They can report back on their observations the following week.

REVIEW ▷

Wordlist

Students work in pairs or small groups to work through the *Wordlist*, checking that they all remember what each word or phrase means, how to pronounce it, and how it was used in the unit. Go through the list carefully with the class.

Academic words review

Students work through the sentences, then check their answers in pairs, and give feedback to the class.

ANSWERS
1 debate   2 labels   3 physical   4 statistics
5 normal

Unit review

Students work through the list alone to decide what they can and can't do. They discuss their answers in pairs, including what they remember from the unit about each point. Finally, open up the discussion to include the whole class. Pay particular attention to any boxes that the students didn't check. Explore with them ways of overcoming any remaining problems.

LISTENING 1	Listening for reasons
LISTENING 2	Listening for contrasts
STUDY SKILL	Getting the most out of discussion
VOCABULARY	Business vocabulary
GRAMMAR	Modal verbs for advice
SPEAKING	Presentation on teamwork

Warm-up

Identify two or three company / brand names on objects in the classroom (**Example:** *on computer equipment, on bags, on writing equipment, on clothing*), and write them on the board. Ask students what they know about the companies (**Example:** *location of head office, size of company, other products made*, whether *growing, or declining* in popularity). Students then call out the names of other companies they can identify through products in the room. In small groups, they discuss their general knowledge of each of these companies. Whole-class feedback could be structured by asking for general opinions on which company is the biggest, best, fastest-growing, best value for money, etc.

Discussion point

Focus the students on the pictures in the infographic, and elicit the vocabulary for the furniture and space they can see (e.g., *cubicle, chair, desk*), adding these words to the board. Then read through the infographic with students, and add additional office or work-related vocabulary to the board (e.g., *office, open space, booth, collaborate, brainstorm*).

If you have worked in different environments, describe some of the places you have worked and what the office area was like, using the vocabulary from the infographic. Students then discuss the questions in pairs or small groups. Monitor and encourage students to ask follow-up questions to find out more. Elicit whole-class feedback. If the *Warm-up* was used, ask what students know about the office spaces of any of the companies mentioned, or any other well-known companies (e.g., *Some of the big tech companies in the U.S. use open spaces, and have game areas for employees to relax and share ideas*).

VIDEO

Before you watch

Ask the students to discuss the questions in pairs. Encourage the students to use follow-up questions to find out more about their partner's answers. During whole-class feedback, keep a tally on the board for questions 1 and 2 to get an overall picture of students' preferences.

While you watch

Warm-up

Write *having a breather* on the board, and elicit student ideas about the meaning of the phrase. Highlight that it is connected to work, and demonstrate the meaning of *breathe*. Once the meaning of the phrase is clear, ask the students to predict how a company might help busy workers traveling around a city to have a breather. Share ideas as a class. Then play the first part of the video (the narrator speaking up to … *and buys an hour*). Students check to see if their ideas were correct.

1 Give students time to read the statements and to work in pairs to predict the order.

2 Students then watch the complete video to check their answers.

ANSWERS
1 c 2 a 3 e 4 b 5 d

See page 108 for the video script.

After you watch

Put students into pairs or groups to discuss the questions. For question 1, ask students to make a note of their ideas in two columns, focusing on the pros and cons of renting an office for an hour. Get feedback on this question, noting their ideas on the board, before students discuss questions 2 and 3. During whole-class feedback, after all questions have been discussed, have a show of hands to indicate who would choose to rent an office by the hour.

LISTENING 1

Work space

A Vocabulary preview

1 Students work alone to match the words in bold to their definitions. Then they compare their answers with a partner's. Go through the answers with the class.

> ANSWERS
>
> **1** d **2** a **3** c **4** b **5** g **6** e **7** h **8** f

2 Students complete the sentences with the words from Exercise 1. Give students time to compare answers with a partner's, before checking as a whole class.

> ANSWERS
>
> **1** seem **2** cubicle **3** I guess **4** emerge **5** set up
> **6** result **7** height **8** effect

Extension activity

Students sit in pairs, back to back. Student A describes the set-up of their living room, dorm room, or study space, identifying what is in the room (e.g., *door, window, furniture, possessions*), and where it is. Student B draws a floor plan of the room. Student A then checks the plan for accuracy, and Student B asks questions about the set-up (e.g., *Why is XX here? How often do you change the set-up? Is there anything you are not happy with? Do you have plans to change it?*).

B Before you listen

Activating prior knowledge

Focus the students on the picture, and give them time to discuss the questions. Monitor and encourage students to extend their answers. Ask pairs to report back the most interesting point from their discussion of each question.

Exam tip

Speaking tests often require candidates to demonstrate skills on several levels. The first level is often descriptive, involving giving information about what can be seen in a picture (i.e., question 1 in the *Before you listen* exercise). Other levels include expressing personal preference (question 2), and talking on a broader, more general level (question 3). Students should practice identifying the type of skill required by each question, and making sure they bring that element of language function into their answer.

C Global listening

Listening for subtopics

Tell students they are going to listen to two students discussing research into useful workspace in offices. Before listening, ask students to provide a definition for each of the working environments on the list (**Example:** *open-plan spaces = large rooms where several people work, with no dividing walls between desks*). Students then listen and number the types of space mentioned.

AUDIO SCRIPT

 Track 3.1

ALEX: Hey Dan. Did you finish your research on the most useful workspace in offices?

DAN: Hi Alex. I did look at different ways offices are set up for work. Do you want to share ideas?

ALEX: Sure, what type of workspace did you focus on?

DAN: I mostly looked at closed office spaces. The reason is that I read a lot about cubicles. I've never had a cubicle, have you?

ALEX: No. I'm from Japan. In Japan, more offices are open-plan. So that's what I decided to research. It seems they work well for big companies that have a lot of employees. I guess you can fit more people into an open workspace. Smaller companies don't need to worry as much. Having said that, closed offices are more expensive, so maybe smaller businesses looking to save money should consider them …

DAN: More expensive … I didn't know that. In the United States, a lot of offices are closed. Workers have their own space. Most employers and employees seem to like the effect on how much work they get done. It's supposed to be easier to have ideas since it's quieter. Most research shows that too much noise, you know, made by colleagues, keeps workers from their jobs.

ALEX: According to my research, closed offices aren't as good because people can't work together as easily. As a result, it has a negative impact on the amount of work that is done. Although it might be quieter and easier to get on with work, if workers don't talk to each other, then there probably aren't as many new ideas, or sales, or results! Open-plan offices, where everyone is in the same room, are better. Open-plan offices are really just one large room with a lot of desks. In Japanese open-plan offices, for example, even the manager works in the same room. As a result, everyone is working together as a team to improve the company's goals.

DAN: Why?

ALEX: Since everyone, no matter what level they are, works in the same space, and in fact, research shows that employees in open-plan offices are more confident in sharing their ideas. Therefore, they are better communicators. And the result is them working better together.

DAN: I read some background information on closed offices. It seems that they are always changing. For example, the height of cubicle walls has changed a lot over time. I guess shorter walls make the workspace more like an open-plan office. It seems a lot of workers in American offices like to have lunch together, but they don't want to share office space. That seems strange, doesn't it?

ALEX: Not really. You'd think people working together would want to discuss things. What if you have a question? Open-plan spaces are better because you can ask right away.

DAN: Maybe. But, think about the issues a manager might have to discuss. A lot of those issues are secret. Because of this, I think closed offices are the better option. But maybe there's a compromise. Perhaps a manager should "earn" a private office, while lower-grade employees work in the open space.

ALEX: Ah, I see what you mean. You're suggesting a combination of open and closed office space within the same office. That could be quite successful—some spaces could be shared for meetings or conferences while other spaces can be used for independent work or higher-level employees.

DAN: Yes, that's a really good idea. OK, I think we have enough to discuss in class tomorrow.

ANSWERS
1 open-plan spaces   2 closed offices
3 cubicles   4 desks   5 shared spaces
6 combination of office space

D Close listening
Listening for reasons

Give students time to read through the *Listening for reasons* box. Then, with books closed, ask students *Why is it useful to listen for reasons?* (**Answer:** *to get more information on the main point*), and *What should you listen for?* (**Answer:** *signal words that indicate reasons*). Then ask students to recall the signal words from the skills box (**Answer:** *The reason is …, Because of this …, Therefore …, Consequently, …*).

1 Students read through the reasons listed. Check understanding of *hard feelings* (**Answer:** *problems between people, like being angry or upset*). Ask students to predict which reason supports having an open office space, and which supports having a closed space. Students then listen to the discussion again, and match the reasons to the types of space.

AUDIO SCRIPT
 Track 3.1

ANSWERS
1 O   2 C   3 O   4 O   5 C

2 Students work in pairs to review the table, and predict how to complete it. Provide support, if required, by writing the answers on the board in a random order. Students then listen to the discussion and check their ideas.

ANSWERS
1 people   2 less   3 more   4 less   5 workers
6 less   7 more   8 more   9 together

E Critical thinking

Students have considered some general pros and cons of open-plan work spaces. The critical thinking questions in this section require the students to evaluate the suitability of such a space in specific circumstances (i.e., for *doctors, lawyers, bosses*). In each case, the students are required to consider the specific circumstances and requirements of each situation, and assess if such a work space is suitable. Going from the general to the specific, along with assessment in relation to key criteria (the requirements for medical appointments), are important aspects of critical thinking.

Prior to answering the questions, students work alone to make a note of the specific requirements for doctors and lawyers, and bosses in general (e.g., *for doctors—privacy to do a medical examination*). Then students discuss the questions in groups. Ask each group to report their conclusions to the class.

STUDY SKILLS

Getting the most out of discussion

Warm-up

Write *Good group members in discussions* … in the middle of the board. Then write *Do* on one side, and *Don't* on the other. Students work in pairs to think of examples of effective behavior and actions of group members, and also behavior and actions which could have a negative effect on the group. Encourage students to think about *before*, *during*, and *after* a discussion. Invite feedback as a whole class, and add the students' ideas to the board. Identify which ideas connect (e.g., *Do—share ideas / Don't—talk when someone else is talking*).

Students read through the information in the *Getting the most out of discussion* box. If the *Warm-up* was used, ask students to compare their ideas with those in the box.

1   Students work in pairs to discuss the questions. After a few minutes, put pairs together to form small groups, and ask the students to explain to the other pair what their partner said to them. Encourage students to develop this section into a discussion through the use of follow-up questions, and by sharing experiences.

2   Highlight that the sentences need either reasons or examples to complete them. Ask students to identify which is which (**Answer:** *reason—1, 2, 4, and 6; example—3 and 5*). Give students time to complete the sentences on their own, before sharing their ideas with their partner or group.

LISTENING 2

A big business
A Vocabulary preview

1   Students work alone to match the words to the definitions. Ask students to check in pairs, and then check as a class.

> **ANSWERS**
> **1** a **2** e **3** f **4** d **5** b **6** c **7** h **8** g

Extension activity

On the board write the following stress patterns: o O o / o o O / O o / o o / O O / O. Students work together to match the words from Exercise 1 to the stress patterns. Encourage students to say the words aloud, and experiment with moving the stress around in the word. A useful way to recognize the correct stress pattern is often to hear the word with the incorrect stress. (**Answers:** o O o— *achievement, efficient*; o o O—*introduce*; O o—*friendship*; o O—*allow, create*; O O—*part-time*; O *sales*.)

2   Read out the sentences and make a "beep" sound, or knock on the table for each blank. Students work in pairs to decide on the correct word. To make this more challenging, students can do this with books closed, recalling the words from Exercise 1. Students then check their answers with another pair.

> **ANSWERS**
> **1** achievement   **2** introduce   **3** create   **4** efficient
> **5** part-time   **6** friendships   **7** sales   **8** allow

3   Students discuss the questions in pairs. Then put pairs together to form small groups. Tell the groups to: decide on the biggest achievement of all the group members; come to an agreement on whether it is a good idea to form a friendship with your boss; write a list of the top three reasons for choosing to work part-time. Monitor the activity and help with vocabulary where needed.

Extension activity

Students work in pairs to write questions for the other words in bold from Exercise 1 (e.g., *Would you like to work in* **sales***?*). Students then change partners and ask and answer their questions. Alternatively, the whole class could mingle, and the students could conduct a survey using their questions (Yes / No questions are easier to manage for a survey activity.)

B Before you listen
Activating prior knowledge

1   Students discuss the questions in pairs. As well as benefits, students can also discuss the disadvantages of big companies for workers. Have the class give feedback.

2   Write *Starbucks* in the middle of the board. Students work as a class to share their knowledge about the company. Build up the ideas in a mind map on the board around the central title. You could introduce sub-categories coming off the central topic if students need more support (e.g., *country, product, customers, workers*, etc.).

Extra research task

As a take-home activity, students research and produce a mind map for another well-known company. This can be started in class, with students working together to share their knowledge about a company. For information they don't know, they write questions (e.g., *How many people work for this company?*). The research is then done outside of class, and the mind map completed.

C Global listening
Listening for main ideas

Give students time to read through the questions before listening. At this point, students could predict the answers. Students then listen to the complete audio, and compare answers at the end. For classes needing more support, play the audio in two or three sections, allowing students to compare answers after each section. Go through the answers with the class.

AUDIO SCRIPT

 Track 3.2

Good morning, class. I know many of you are probably in this class because you want to start your own business. Starting a business is a lot of hard work, but a lot of big businesses today all started as little businesses.

Today, we will talk about Starbucks. This may surprise you, but Starbucks started as a small company. The first Starbucks opened in Seattle, Washington, in the United States before a lot of you were even born … 1971. The good news is that it was started by students. Students just like you. The three went to college together at the University of San Francisco. The company had to do a lot of things to become a big business, but now it has stores in over 72 countries! So what did Starbucks do to keep their business successful after it grew?

A company that big has to have a lot of workers. The main office in Seattle has over 3,500 employees. How do you make sure employees are happy? In the case of Starbucks, they believe employees come first. The company cares about its workers. One of the presidents of Starbucks started this idea. He believed that if the company cared about its workers, then the workers would care about the customers, and that this would result in the company's success.

Starbucks also believes that workers should be friends. Many of the workers form friendships with each other. This usually results in workers being friendly towards customers, too. Consequently, the customers are happy, and the company is popular.

Another thing Starbucks does for its employees is encourage communication. A group of people work together to deliver your order. Good communication between them leads to good customer service and should increase sales.

Starbucks is also known for its openness. What do I mean by that? A lot of workers are afraid to talk to their bosses and would never argue with the boss. One of Starbucks' presidents introduced something called an "open forum." In these sessions, workers are allowed to ask questions to the bosses. The workers take advantage of this. Because of this, employees feel that they work at an open and friendly place.

Lastly, Starbucks has a policy that includes everyone. It doesn't matter who you are or where you're from. Anyone can work at Starbucks! Again, this makes the workers very happy which results in happy customers.

Of course, Starbucks offers its employees some good benefits, too. For example, they provide healthcare benefits to both their part-time and full-time workers. One thing you may all appreciate is that Starbucks offers full tuition reimbursement through its College Achievement Plan. Employees are also able to own shares in the company and save in retirement plans.

To conclude, let's look at Starbucks' values. The first value listed is "creating a culture of warmth and belonging, where everyone is welcome." When you think about it, Starbucks has very loyal customers. I have friends who go to Starbucks every day and I know some of my students go to Starbucks every night to study. It seems to live up to this value by making its employees and its customers very happy. Because of these values, a small company grew into a very successful big company. Other companies can learn from Starbucks.

ANSWERS
1 b **2** c **3** a **4** c **5** c

D Close listening

Listening for contrasts

1   Give students time to read through the skills box, and then model the pronunciation of the words. Students then listen to the four sentences from *A big business* and circle the words they hear. Students check their answers in pairs, and then listen again. Go through the answers with the class.

AUDIO SCRIPT

 Track 3.3

1   It seems to live up to this value by making its employees and its customers very happy.

2   The company cares about its workers.

3   Many of the workers form friendships with each other.

4   It doesn't matter who you are.

ANSWERS

1 live   **2** its   **3** each   **4** matter

---

2   Give students time to read through the flowchart of the presentation. Students can complete any answers they can recall, and predict the others. Students then listen to the presentation, then check and complete their answers.

AUDIO SCRIPT

 Track 3.2

ANSWERS

1 1971   **2** employees   **3** customers
4 communication   **5** customer service
6 good benefits   **7** Achievement

E Critical thinking

Elicit the ways *Starbucks* motivates its workforce (**Possible answers:** *encourages workers to make friends with each other, believes in open communication, "Open Forums," good benefits for full-time and part-time workers, college tuition fees paid*). Students discuss other ways to motivate a workforce and list their ideas. During whole-class feedback, build up a list of the students' ideas on the board.

In groups, students review and discuss the list on the board from question 1. Encourage the groups to identify the three most effective ways and three least effective ways to motivate a workforce.

PRONUNCIATION

Pronunciation for listening
Continuing speech

Warm-up

With books closed, ask students what they would order from *Starbucks*. Elicit three items and write them on the board (e.g., *coffee, water, cake*). Read out the list with rising intonation on the first two items and falling intonation on the final item. Exaggerate the intonation and use hand movements to highlight. Elicit the difference between the way you said the first two items, and the final item. Then elicit what the falling intonation indicates (**Answer:** *that the list has finished*). Now say the list again, this time with rising intonation on all the items, including the final one. Elicit that this indicates to the listener that the list has not come to an end. Ask students whether the same feature exists in their own language.

Students then work in pairs to list items (e.g., *food items, sports, days of the week*), either choosing to "finish" the list, or not. If the partner thinks the student has finished the list, they remain silent. If they think the list is unfinished, they add another item to finish (i.e., with falling intonation).

1 Students read through the *Continuing speech* box. Model the sentences for them. Students then listen to the sentences and decide if the intonation rises, or falls. Highlight that the main movement in the intonation is usually at the end of the phrase.

AUDIO SCRIPT

🎧 **Track 3.4**

1 Have you ever been to a Starbucks?
2 Good communication between them leads to good customer service, and should increase sales.
3 Because of this, employees feel that they work at an open and friendly place.
4 It doesn't matter who you are.

> ANSWERS
> 1 rise   2 fall   3 fall   4 rise

2 Students listen and repeat. Drill the phrases as a whole class, and then allow students time to take turns in pairs listening to the phrases, saying them, and giving feedback to their partner.

AUDIO SCRIPT

🎧 **Track 3.4**

3 Read through the instructions together, and ask what students should do if they want more time to speak (**Answer:** *finish with rising intonation*). Then ask students to discuss the questions in pairs. Monitor and encourage use of rising and falling intonation.

Extension activity

Make a note of effective use of intonation you hear while monitoring in Exercise 3. Also note places where intonation could have been used. Add these phrases to the board, and ask students to identify the appropriate intonation pattern.

VOCABULARY

Vocabulary development
Business vocabulary

1 Students work alone to match the words to their definitions. Ask students to check the words and definitions in pairs. Have the class give feedback.

> ANSWERS
> 1 a   2 c   3 b   4 d   5 h   6 g   7 f   8 e

2 Students work alone to identify the correct words. Ask students to check in pairs, and then check as a class.

> ANSWERS
> 1 suggestion   2 realistic   3 double   4 unemployment
> 5 triple   6 realistic

Extension activity

Students work in small groups to come up with three top tips for starting your own business. Organize this as a pyramid discussion. First, each student works alone to make a list of four tips. Then, they work in a group, share their tips, and try to agree on three. Tell the groups you will award a point for the use of each word from the *Vocabulary* section when they report their ideas to the class.

Academic words

1 Students work alone to choose the correct definition. Then ask students to check in pairs. Drill the words as a whole class and individually.

ANSWERS

1 b 2 b 3 b 4 a 5 b 6 b 7 a 8 a

2 Students work alone to complete the sentences with the words from Exercise 1. Ask students to compare their answers in pairs, and then go through the answers with the class.

ANSWERS

1 indicate 2 specify 3 evolving 4 definite
5 revision 6 academic 7 policy 8 paragraph

SPEAKING >

Speaking model

Read through the information with the aims for this section. Highlight that the different parts of the *Speaking* section build towards the final task.

A Model

1 Focus on the set of notes, and elicit the punctuation and writing features which indicate these are notes (**Possible answers:** *bullet points, dashes, no periods, incomplete sentences*). Then ask students to read through the set of notes, and complete the summary with the correct words. Check answers as a class to establish and clarify the problem, asking students to explain it to you in their own words.

ANSWERS

1 sales 2 worse 3 communication 4 less

2 Give the students time to read through the presentation. They should then identify the suggestions, and the words and phrases that introduce these. After comparing answers in pairs, go through the answers with the class.

ANSWERS

One suggestion is that …   They should also …

B Discuss

Students discuss the questions in pairs. They then work in small groups, with different students, sharing their suggestions. The group should decide on the best alternative solution, and report this to the class. Collect the ideas on the board, and ask students to try to agree on the best alternative suggestion overall.

GRAMMAR >

Modal verbs for advice

Warm-up

With books closed, describe a simple work-related problem to students (**Example:** *One of your colleagues has very loud personal phone calls at his desk.*) Ask the students for their advice. Reformulate it as necessary, and add it to the board using *should* for one definite piece of advice, and *could …, or … could* for more than one suggestion. Also add suggestions with *might,* and *may* (or the negative forms). Thank the students for their advice, and say which you are going to follow. Then ask if anyone has a similar work or study related problem. Elicit advice from the rest of the class for this problem, using the examples on the board to model the language in the students' responses.

Students read through the *Modal verbs for advice* box. If the *Warm-up* was used, ask students to explain the difference between the use of *should* and *could* (**Answer:** *one main suggestion versus more than one*).

1 Students work alone to complete the sentences with a modal verb. Ask them to then compare their answers in pairs, reminding them that more than one answer may be possible. Go through the answers with the class.

POSSIBLE ANSWERS

1 shouldn't 2 could / may / might 3 might / may
4 should 5 could / may / might 6 should
7 should / may / might 8 could / might

2 Highlight that the errors contained in the sentences could be either errors of meaning, or errors of form. Students correct the errors alone, and then compare their answers with a partner's. Go through the answers with the class.

ANSWERS

1 should 2 sell 3 have 4 want
5 could 6 shouldn't

Speaking skill
Turn-taking

Warm-up

With books closed, ask students to think about when they are in a group discussion. Ask them which phrases they could use to say they would like to make the first point / interrupt / ask the opinion of others / say they would like to finish their point. Elicit different suggestions, and reformulate into correct structures. Then give students time to read through the *Turn-taking* box, and study the phrases. Ask students to close the books again, and divide the class into two teams. Have a competition to see which team can recall the phrases accurately from the box. Award a point for each correct phrase.

1   Students read through the skills box and then match the function to the phrases. Ask students to check their answers in pairs, and then practice the turns. Monitor and give some help with pausing and clear delivery. This will lead into the coming *Pronunciation* focus.

> **ANSWERS**
> **1** interrupting   **2** saying you are not finished
> **3** encouraging others to speak

2 and 3   Give students time to read through the turns they need to follow, and assign their roles. They then have the conversation. Monitor and make a note of successful language use in relation to the speaking skill, and also language that needs reformulating. After the first conversation, invite whole-class feedback, analyzing some of the examples you have collected. Students then switch roles, and have another conversation using the same turns.

PRONUNCIATION >

Pronunciation for speaking
Chunking a presentation

Extra support: Give the opening of a presentation to the students (e.g., the model in the Student Book). However, do not include any chunking (i.e., pauses and main stresses). Elicit the problem and the effect on the audience (**Example answer:** *The voice will sound boring, and the ideas will be difficult to follow.*). Give students time to read through the *Chunking a presentation* box. Ask students to explain the information in the box in their own words.

1 and 2   Students listen to the presentation and mark the pauses. Play the audio in chunks, allowing the students to compare their pause marks as the presentation progresses.

When they have finished Exercise 1, elicit from students that the main syllable in the most important words (the information words) tends to be stressed. Give them time top predict which syllables these will be, indicating with a light mark on the page. Students then listen again, correcting and confirming their predictions as they go.

AUDIO SCRIPT

 Track 3.5

My presentation today is about how Julio and Marcus can improve things at work so that they can start making more money for the business.

Julio has said that the reason why he is having problems at work is because he has a family. A lot of people have babies and families and they still have to work.

People need to be able to balance their work lives with their family lives. Julio and Marcus need to establish ways to overcome this. One suggestion is that they have a split schedule. In other words, Marcus could work earlier in the morning because Julio needs to come in later. Then Julio could work later in the evening.

They would then work the same number of hours, and Marcus would not be doing double the work. Julio has to take the late shift so that he can sleep later in the morning. I think if they do this, they will both do the same amount of work. They should also specify a time to meet in the middle of each day so that they can make sure they are getting everything done.

In conclusion, communicating and changing the schedule would be an easy way to make both of them happy, and help increase company profits. Profits could be checked on a bi-annual basis to make sure this new policy works.

My presentation today | is about how Julio and Marcus | can improve things at work | so that they can start making more money | for the business.

Julio has said | that the reason why | he is having problems at work | is because he has a family. | A lot of people have babies and families | and they still have to work.

People need | to be able to balance | their work lives | with their family lives. | Julio and Marcus need to establish ways | to overcome this. | One suggestion is that | they have a split schedule. | In other words, | Marcus could work earlier in the morning | because Julio needs to come in later. | Then, | Julio could work later in the evening.

They would then work the same number of hours | and Marcus would not be doing double the work. | Julio has to take the late shift | so that he can sleep later in the morning. | I think, | if they do this, | they will both do the same amount of work. | They should also specify a time to meet | in the middle of each day | so that they can make sure they are getting everything done.

In conclusion, | communicating and changing the schedule | would be an easy way to make both of them happy, | and help increase company profits. | Profits could be checked on a bi-annual basis | to make sure this new policy works.

3 Students compare their scripts in pairs, and then practice delivering parts of the speech to each other.

SPEAKING ▷

Speaking task

Warm-up

Allow students time to review the unit, both the information, and the language points. Give a time limit, and tell them there will then be a series of mini-quizzes. You can choose the focus of these, as appropriate for your class (**Examples:** *vocabulary / Starbucks / giving advice / how to interrupt / etc.*). When the review time is finished, students organize their teams, and think of a team name. Then run the quizzes, giving points accordingly.

Brainstorm and plan

Read through the task with students. Then give students time to read through the report notes. Check the meaning of vocabulary as necessary.

Put students into groups of three, and ask them to rank the problems in order of importance. Remind them that they need to focus on the aim as given (*of turning the business around, working together as a team, and improving employee satisfaction*) to do this. Students could first reduce the list to around ten items, and from there, select the top three.

Once the top three problems have been identified, students focus on solutions, brainstorming suggestions for each problem. Monitor and encourage students to think creatively at this point. They can always discard ideas later.

Students then prepare to present their ideas, deciding who will talk about each problem and solution.

Speak and share

Students present their ideas to another group. Remind them of the language to use, and to focus on clear delivery of their ideas with pausing and stress. Monitor and note effective and less effective use of target language from the unit. Use this for whole-class feedback, praising effective use of the target language.

Both groups then evaluate the ideas they shared, using the questions for guidance. Monitor and encourage reflection, prompting students to identify examples to support their views.

Reflect

Students discuss the answers in pairs. In whole-class feedback, ask students to share any interesting cases they discussed.

REVIEW ▷

Wordlist

Students work in pairs or small groups to work through the *Wordlist*, checking that they all remember what each word or phrase means, how to pronounce it, and how it was used in the unit. Go through the list carefully with the class.

Academic words review

Students work through the sentences, check their answers in pairs, and then give feedback to the class.

ANSWERS
1 policy 2 paragraph 3 strategy
4 academic 5 indicate

Unit review

Students work through the list alone to decide what they can and can't do. They discuss their answers in pairs, including what they remember from the unit about each point. Finally, open up the discussion to include the whole class. Pay particular attention to any boxes that the students didn't check. Explore with them ways of overcoming any remaining problems.

4 TRENDS

LISTENING 1	Listening for dates
LISTENING 2	Listening for time signals
STUDY SKILL	Time management
VOCABULARY	Synonyms and antonyms
GRAMMAR	Simple past: ordering past events
SPEAKING	Describing a timeline

Warm-up

With books closed, have a "timeline" quiz as a class. Draw a timeline on the board. Mark the year 1850 at one end and now at the other. Then mark 1900, 1950, and 2000 on the line in approximately the correct position. Ask students to work in small groups, and make one copy of the line for their group. Then, if possible, show images of different types of cars, or describe them. Ask students to mark the year each type of car was invented. Check answers and award points for approximately correct answers, and the right order of all the items. Student groups could come to the board to mark their answers on the timeline there, using different colors for each group, for example. Ask students to open their books and look at the timeline of the telephone.

Discussion point

Students discuss the questions in pairs. When eliciting whole-class feedback, elicit their reactions to the timeline, and also to the statistic about cell phone ownership (e.g., *Are you surprised? Why? What did you think before you read this?*).

Extension activity

Do a mini show-and-tell with your cell phone. Show it to the class, and talk about it for two minutes (e.g., Explain how long you have had it, why you chose it, the good things and bad things about it, etc.). Students then do the same in pairs with their own cell phones / tablets.

VIDEO

Who's to blame?
Before you watch

If not covered in the *Warm-up* stage, ask students whether they know when the first car was invented (**Answer:** *1896*) and ask generally about the development of cars over the past 100 years. This should lead to the recent development of driverless cars (the topic of the video), and perhaps to the future development of flying cars.

Students match the words to the correct definitions, and then discuss how each phrase might appear in the video.

> ANSWERS
> 1 c 2 a 3 e 4 b 5 d

While you watch

Give students time to read through the sentences before watching. At this stage, they can predict the correct answers. Then play the video for students to watch and confirm their predictions.

> ANSWERS
> 1 safer 2 do crash sometimes 3 normal traffic
> 4 might be 5 who or what is to blame

See page 108 for the video script.

After you watch

Put the students into small groups to discuss the questions. Monitor and encourage the students to ask each other follow-up questions to extend the discussion, and explore each other's answers (e.g., *Why do you say that? Has your view changed? Are there any disadvantages?*). Invite whole-class feedback. Put students' ideas for advantages of driverless cars in a column on the board. Then elicit disadvantages. Have a class vote to see who is in favor of driverless cars.

Car safety
A Vocabulary preview

Warm-up

Show a picture of a car, and elicit all the related vocabulary known by students, writing it in a column on the board. Check pronunciation and mark word stress as necessary.

1   Students work alone to match the words to the definitions. Ask students to check in pairs, and then check as a class. Check pronunciation and highlight the three compound words (*airbag, anti-lock brake,* and *seat belt*). Remind students that compound words tend to have roughly equal stress. Model and drill the pronunciation of these words.

ANSWERS

1 h   **2** c   **3** d   **4** a   **5** b   **6** g   **7** f   **8** e

2   Ask students to complete the sentences with the correct form of the words from Exercise 1. Ask students to check in pairs, and then check as a class.

ANSWERS

1 passengers   **2** anti-lock brakes   **3** invented
4 wheels   **5** seat belts   **6** regulations
7 airbag   **8** rear

3   Students discuss the questions with a partner.

Extension activity

In pairs, students write questions for the remaining six words from Exercise 1 (e.g., *Have you ever been in a car when an* **airbag** *filled?*). Students then interview a new partner with the questions. Ask individuals to report back two interesting things they discovered about their new partner.

B Before you listen

Activating prior knowledge

Check the understanding of *safety features*, eliciting an example from the *Vocabulary preview* section (e.g., *airbag, anti-lock brake, seat belt*). Then put students into pairs to discuss the questions. When they have finished, re-organize the students so they work with a new partner, explaining the answers from the previous discussion. In whole-class feedback, ask what safety features were mentioned. Ask also about road regulations designed to increase safety (e.g., *speed limits, signals*).

C Global listening
Listening for key words

Give students time to read through the two questions and ten options. Check vocabulary meaning as required. Students then listen and match three answers to question 1, and two answers to question 2. Allow time for students to compare answers in pairs. Play the audio again in segments, if appropriate for your class. Go through the answers with the class.

Exam skills

This multiple-matching exercise is common in many standardized exams such as IELTS. Students should take any available time before listening to read through the questions and options, identifying key words, and predicting possible answers.

AUDIO SCRIPT
🎧 Track 4.1

ALI: I like our history class. I thought studying history would be boring, but it's not.

JUANITA: Me too, Ali. I didn't think we would get to talk about inventions.

MOSHE: I'm glad our project is going to be about cars, Juanita. Our topic is car safety. Let's get started.

ALI: What should we start with, Moshe? Seat belts?

MOSHE: That's a good idea, Ali. Everyone will be familiar with seat belts. And most research says these benefit drivers the most.

JUANITA: According to my research, seat belts were introduced in 1958. I had no idea they have been around for so long.

MOSHE: In the U.S., seat belts have been a required safety feature since 1968.

JUANITA: Well, since we are on the topic of seat belts, we should mention rear seat belts. That is, seat belts in the back seats of cars. I read that the first seat belt law in the United States required that all vehicles, except buses, have seat belts in all places where a passenger could sit.

ALI: However, most states didn't introduce the law to say you had to wear a seat belt until the 1980s, or 1990s ... 20, or 30 years later.

MOSHE: I read that, too. It was in 1968. But, even though the seat belts were there, passengers were not required to wear them. That didn't happen until ... New York required it in 1984.

ALI: OK, great. What else should we talk about? ... How about brakes? We should definitely mention anti-lock brakes. They were first introduced on airplanes. Then cars started using them in 1966.

JUANITA: What are anti-lock brakes exactly, Ali?

ALI: They prevent the wheels from locking. So when the driver presses the brake, the wheels keep turning automatically and then the car doesn't slide across the ground.

JUANITA: Hmm. OK. Definitely very important, especially in countries where there is a lot of rain or ice.

MOSHE: Next is airbags. The first car produced with an airbag was in 1981. At first, only the driver's side included an airbag. Now, I think a lot of cars have them on both sides. That trend really took off.

JUANITA: Good point, Moshe. I think we should include one more safety item. How about learning what happens when a car crashes? That is a topic many people won't think about. This test is called a crash test. The first crash tests happened in 1994 in Europe.

ALI: They're important. I can't remember which car it was, but when it was first tested in 1996, it didn't do well and people thought it was very unsafe. This proves that people do take safety seriously.

MOSHE: I can't remember the name of the car either, but I know what you're talking about. That car only got one star on the Euro NCAP five-star rating system.

JUANITA: Does anyone know if any cars ever got a five-star rating?

MOSHE: Yes, there was one in 2001.

ALI: That seems like a great place to conclude our presentation…

ANSWERS
1 BDE **2** GI

D Close listening

Listening for dates

Read through the *Listening for dates* box with the students. Model and drill the years given. Write other dates on the board and ask students to say them correctly.

---

1 Give students time to review the timeline, seeing which events it contains. They could try to recall, and / or predict the dates. They then listen again to the discussion to check.

AUDIO SCRIPT

 Track 4.1

ANSWERS
1958 – Seat belts introduced
1966 – Anti-lock brakes introduced
1981 – Airbags introduced
1994 – First crash tests
1966 – First car to get a five-star rating

---

2 Give students time to read the questions and predict the answers. They have heard the discussion twice by this point, so they will probably be able to recall some of the answers. Then play the audio for students to listen, check, and complete their answers.

AUDIO SCRIPT

 Track 4.1

ANSWERS
1 a **2** b **3** b **4** c

E Critical thinking

Critical thinking covers a broad range of skills, often used in a variety of flexible combinations. Here the students have the opportunity to review a previous answer and expand on it, integrating learning from the listening. They then have the opportunity to think creatively (one of the "higher level" critical thinking skills) bringing together practical experience with being a passenger, and / or driver in a car, research, and their own inventive skills.

Students discuss the questions in small groups. Then ask each group to present their safety feature to the class.

STUDY SKILLS

Time management

> **Warm-up**
>
> Write *Time management* on the board, and elicit students' ideas about what the phrase involves. Add their ideas to the board on a mind map. Provide the first level of branches from the central point in the mind map to support students as necessary (e.g., *What? When? How? Why?*).

Read through the *Time management* box with the students. Ask students to expand on each of the bullet points with examples from their own experience, and / or explanations in their own words.

1 Students complete the questionnaire alone. They can then compare answers in a group. If appropriate, ask each group to identify who has the most effective time management skills, and explain why.

2 Explain to students they are going to produce their own to-do list using time management techniques. Ask them to work down through the checklist, checking off each item as they complete it. When they have finished, they compare lists with a partner.

LISTENING 2

Urban sprawl

A Vocabulary preview

Focus the students on the image on page 69, and say it shows an urban sprawl. From this, ask students to define *urban sprawl* (**Possible answer:** *A large area covered by buildings that spreads out from the center of a city*).

1 Students match the words to the definitions. Ask students to check in pairs, and then check as a class.

> **ANSWERS**
> **1** h **2** f **3** e **4** g **5** a **6** b **7** d **8** c

2 Students work together in pairs to decide if the sentences are *T* (True) or *F* (False). Alternatively, you could run this as a group quiz with books closed.

> **ANSWERS**
> **1** T **2** F **3** F **4** T **5** T **6** F **7** T **8** F

B Before you listen

Activating prior knowledge

> **Warm-up**
>
> Describe a city you know to the class without saying which city it is. Use vocabulary from *Vocabulary preview* (e.g., *The population is XX. There are some ancient buildings in the center.*). Students should guess the city, but with each guess they need to justify why they are saying that city (e.g., *Washington, D.C. You said it is the capital of the U.S.A.*). Students can then play the game with a partner.

1 Students discuss the question in pairs. During whole-class feedback, build a list of common features of cities on the board.

2 Copy the diagram onto the board, next to the list of common features, and invite students to come to the board to label the parts in the box. Ask students who live in cities to explain to the class which area of their city they live in in relation to the diagram, and how many of the common features of a city their own city has.

> **ANSWERS**
> blue: central business district   purple: inner city
> green: inner suburbs   yellow: outer suburbs

C Global listening
Listening for main ideas

Give students time to read through the *Glossary*. Model the pronunciation for each word. If extra support is required, ask students to work in pairs to decide how each date is said. Students can also identify the key words in each question (**Possible answers:** *1 begin, 2 start / affect / United States, 3 continue / problem*). Students then listen to *Urban sprawl* and answer the questions.

AUDIO SCRIPT

 Track 4.2

PROFESSOR: Good morning, class. Today, I want to focus on a trend called urban sprawl. I want to begin by discussing some background information about urban sprawl and how it developed in the United States. Essentially, urban sprawl happens when the population of a city spreads to the surrounding areas, known as suburbs, which are outside the city center. The suburbs get bigger and bigger as people move into them. Because of the large number of people, many houses are built in these areas as well as other developments like malls and stores.

STUDENT 1:   How can someone tell where the suburbs start and the city ends? The new areas look like the city, don't they?

PROFESSOR: Good question. It depends on the design. There might be similarities between the outer parts of the city and the suburbs, for example, in terms of the layout of the buildings. But in most cases, they don't look the same. You will find that there are lots of different styles of building within a city, but the suburbs are more likely to have the same style of buildings throughout. In fact, some argue that design inspiration is lost in the suburbs. Not only are there more houses, but they all look the same. Even the malls and stores look similar.

STUDENT 2:   When did this happen? It must be recent. We haven't always had suburbs, right?

PROFESSOR: Most people think urban sprawl is a relatively new concept. Others think it began in the 1950s. However, that's not actually the case. While many of our modern cities have been designed to reduce urban sprawl, it's actually a concept that has been around for many centuries. In fact, urban sprawl has existed as long as cities have existed. Rome is one of the oldest cities in history and was one of the most crowded. At the time of early Rome, almost 3,000 years ago, the population started to spread outward. And it wasn't just Rome. Even before that, in more ancient history, Babylon and China also saw considerable urban sprawl. In more recent times, London experienced its share of urban sprawl—in the 17th and 18th centuries. During that time, the richer citizens started moving away from the city center into the suburbs.

STUDENT 3:   So, where else has urban sprawl been an issue?

PROFESSOR: Well, in the early 1900s, urban sprawl began affecting North America, the United States, in particular. Later, in 1918, a rapid increase in immigration after World War I resulted in greater urban growth. Around the same time, the number of affordable cars meant that middle-class people could live further away, but still travel to work in the city center. As a result, suburbs started growing around large cities. This meant that millions of new homes were built, and cities grew more, increasing the amount of urban sprawl.

STUDENT 4:   What about more recently? It seems we are still seeing urban sprawl today.

PROFESSOR: You're right. Later, in the 1970s, the sprawl continued—by this point it was becoming a social phenomenon that had an impact on how our living and working spaces changed. Some cities doubled in land size, but city center populations decreased. Furthermore, cities saw more and more suburbs spreading further and further away from the center. In fact, today, inner-city populations are at an all-time low. Some reasons for this include: you can buy more for your money in the suburbs, there are more green open spaces, and it's generally a quieter area to live.

ANSWERS
1 b **2** b **3** a

D Close listening
Listening for time signals

With books closed, ask students how the unit started, and what item they looked at in relation to a timeline (*phones*). Elicit the information on a timeline (*date and event*), and why timelines might be good for making notes (**Possible answer:** *a clear visual record of key events in the order they happened*).

1   Read through the *Listening for time signals* box with students. Give students time to review the timeline they are going to complete. Ask if students can recall events that happened for different places on the timeline. Students then listen again to *Urban sprawl,* and add details to the timeline. Allow time for students to compare and complete their timelines after listening.

AUDIO SCRIPT

 Track 4.2

> **POSSIBLE ANSWERS**
> Ancient times = Babylon and China saw considerable urban sprawl
> Nearly 3,000 years ago = early Roman population started to spread outward
> 17th and 18th centuries = London experienced urban sprawl
> Early 1900s = urban sprawl began in the U.S.
> 1918 = immigration resulted in greater urban growth
> 1940s and 1950s = government policies contributed to urban sprawl
> 1970s = urban sprawl became a social phenomenon
> Present day = inner city populations are at all-time lows

2   Students answer the questions using their timelines. They can then work with a new partner asking and answering questions about the development of urban sprawl.

> **ANSWERS**
> **1** a   **2** b   **3** a

E Critical thinking

Students discuss the questions with a partner. For question 1, ask them to create a two-column table to makes notes of advantages and disadvantages of urban sprawl. To answer question 2, students can use this table as the focus for discussion, with students considering how they are affected by both the advantages and disadvantages of urban sprawl.

Pronunciation for listening
Sounds in dates and numbers

Read through the *Sounds in dates and numbers* box with students, modeling the dates, and drilling as a whole class and individually. Remind students that they should also consider their own world knowledge when assessing whether what they thought they heard is correct (e.g., *Did more people fly in airplanes in 1915 or 1950? 1950 is obvious from world knowledge.*).

1   Play the audio while students listen and circle the date they hear. Allow time for students to compare their answers before playing the audio again.

AUDIO SCRIPT

 Track 4.3
1   Others think it began in the 1960s.
2   In 1918, a rapid increase in immigration after World War I resulted in greater urban growth.
3   Later, in the 1970s, the sprawl continued.

> **ANSWERS**
> **1** the 1960s   **2** 1918   **3** the 1970s

2   Students work in pairs, with one saying and the other pointing to a date on the timeline.

> **Extension activity**
>
> Say a series of dates and numbers, and students listen and note them down. Award one point for every correct answer. Students then work in pairs. One student in each pair writes a list of ten dates and numbers. They do not show this to their partner, but read them out one by one as their partner writes them. They then swap roles. The winner is the person who gets more dates and numbers correct.

Vocabulary development
Synonyms and antonyms

With books closed, write the words *large*, *big*, and *small* on the board. Ask students to explain the different relationships between the words (**Answer:** *big and large have similar meanings = synonyms; big / large and small have opposite meanings = antonyms*). Ask students if they can think of words with similar relationships. Add their ideas to the board.

Read through the *Synonyms and antonyms* box with students and check the meanings of the example words used.

1   Students work with a partner to complete the chart. Go through the answers with the class, and ask students to note the word stress on the words, and drill the pronunciation.

ANSWERS
boring – uninteresting – exciting
crowded – busy – quiet
modern – new – ancient
safe – secure – dangerous
dirty – filthy – clean
expensive – valuable – cheap
famous – well-known – unknown

Extension activity

Students need to spend short bursts of time, at regular intervals, learning new vocabulary. Build this into class time by having pop quizzes. At this point in the class, ask students to spend a few minutes studying the chart from Exercise 1. Put students into pairs. Each partner should text the other by saying one of the three words, and asking for the other two from memory. They should take turns testing each other on the whole vocabulary set.

2   Students work alone to complete the paragraph with antonyms where appropriate. Go through the answers with the class.

ANSWERS
2 modern   **5** cheap

Academic words

1   Students work alone to match the sentences to the correct definitions. Ask students to check in pairs, and at the same time to identify the word stress pattern of the academic words. Go through the answers with the class, and invite students to come to the board to add the words to the correct stress pattern.

ANSWERS
1 h   **2** e   **3** c   **4** f   **5** b   **6** g   **7** a   **8** d

2   Students discuss the questions in pairs, reporting back the most interesting answers to the class.

Extension activity

Students work alone to write statements expressing their own views using the words from Exercise 1. They should then mingle and check each sentence off when they find someone who agrees with it (e.g., *The government should spend a **considerable** amount of money making our cities safer. Do you agree?*).

Speaking model

Warm-up

With books closed, write *Dubai* on the board. Alternatively, show the class some images of the city, and ask students where it is. Then elicit everything students know about the place. Once some facts about the present have been written up on the board, focus the students on the city's past. It is highly likely that less will be known about Dubai's past. In this case, help students out with keywords (*pearls / fire / trade*, etc.). After they have done this, write some of the key past dates on the board, and ask students to guess what happened in each year. You could provide the events, and invite students to match them up to the years.

A Analyze

Give students time to read through the model, and to choose the best words to complete the summary.

ANSWERS
1 history   2 ask questions

B Discuss

Students discuss the questions in pairs. Monitor the exercise, and elicit some answers in open class at the end.

Extra research activity

Highlight the *Glossary* for the word *pearl*, and elicit the details from the presentation about pearl diving. Then assign a take-home activity for students to research the topic of pearl diving in Dubai, and produce a timeline for it. These can then be presented in small groups during the next class.

GRAMMAR >

Simple past: ordering past events

Read through the *Simple past: ordering past events* box with students. Ask students to read through the skills box again in their own time. As they do this, write the following sentences on the board: *I moved to the city after I left college. / I moved to the city because I had a new job there. / I moved to the city so that I could make more money.* Ask students to use the information from the box to explain the differences between the sentences, focusing on the relationship between the first clause and second (**Answers:** *The first is time sequence, the second is a reason, and the third is a result.*)

1 Students work alone to complete the sentences with the simple past of the verbs in parentheses. Go through the answers with the class.

ANSWERS
1 researched   2 lived   3 was, ended   4 happened

2 Students work alone to complete the sentences. They then compare answers in pairs before checking as a whole class.

ANSWERS
1 so that   2 because   3 since   4 in order to

SPEAKING >

Speaking skill
Asking for clarification and repetition

Give students time to read through the *Asking for clarification and repetition* box. Model the pronunciation of the phrases for them. Emphasize the stress, which students can mark, and show how some of the words contract (e.g., *What'd'ya mean?*). Ask students to practice the phrases in pairs.

Students work in groups of three. Give all three students time to read through the information. They should check any language they are unclear on, and identify possible details which could be clarified, or repeated. One student should then read out the first paragraph, and the other two ask for clarification and repetition. Monitor and make a note of effective and less effective language use, focusing on the key phrases from this section. Go through the answers with the class, with students correcting and improving the language samples you present.

Students then change roles and use the second paragraph. Provide feedback at the end on any improved language use.

Extension activity

With books closed, write the four categories on the board: *Asking for clarification; Giving clarification; Asking for repetition; Repeating yourself.* Elicit the differences from the students, and then ask them to identify phrases from the speaking model which do each of these things.

PRONUNCIATION ▶

Pronunciation for speaking
Stress in phrases connected with *and*

Read through the *Stress in phrases connected with* and box with the students. Model the language and highlight how *and* is reduced to *n* at times. Elicit that in English, we usually stress the information words in a sentence, and because *and* (except in special circumstances such as for contrast) carries little information, it is not stressed.

1 Students work in pairs to identify the stressed words in each sentence. Encourage the students to say the sentences out loud to identify the patterns, and to listen to each other. They should, however, avoid a "reading aloud" voice, and focus on trying to say the sentences naturally.

2 Play the audio for students to check their answers. Then give students time to practice. Monitor and assist as necessary.

AUDIO SCRIPT

🎧 **Track 4.4**

1 The process of buying a car isn't usually quick and easy.
2 There are positives and negatives to owning a car; it's not all good.
3 I like peace and quiet, so electric cars are my favorite.
4 Pinar would not tell us where she is going to college. We will have to wait and see.
5 She's very talented; she gets top grades in arts and sciences.

ANSWERS

1 The process of buying a car isn't usually <u>quick</u> and <u>easy</u>.
2 There are <u>positives</u> and <u>negatives</u> to owning a car; it's not all good.
3 I like <u>peace</u> and <u>quiet</u>, so electric cars are my favorite.
4 Pinar would not tell us where she is going to college. We will have to <u>wait</u> and <u>see</u>.
5 She's very talented; she gets top grades in <u>arts</u> and <u>sciences</u>.

SPEAKING ▶

Speaking task

Give the students time to review the unit. Read through the task first, and then tell students to make notes of useful ideas and language from the unit that might help them with it.

Brainstorm and plan

Students work in pairs to brainstorm a list of events that could be included on a timeline about a city (e.g., *the date it was founded, key historical dates, the date it got a public transportation system, date the local soccer team won a significant game*). Highlight that students shouldn't write the actual facts at this stage, but they should focus instead on the type of information that could be included.

Students then work alone to complete their own timeline, doing extra research as appropriate to find out the key facts. Students then continue to prepare alone by writing simple past questions to describe their timelines. Put students into pairs, and ask them to work together to review and revise their sentences, as necessary.

Speak and share

Students work with a new partner. They present their timelines while their partner asks for repetition and clarification as required, in order to make notes on the information on the timeline. They then change roles.

Students then report back to their original partner, using their notes to share interesting information about the city they heard about.

Reflect

Students consider the question alone, making notes on their ideas. They then share these ideas in a small group.

Wordlist

Students work in pairs or small groups to work through the *Wordlist*, checking that they all remember what each word or phrase means, how to pronounce it, and how it was used in the unit. Go through the list carefully with the class.

Academic words review

Students work through the sentences, check their answers in pairs, and give feedback to the class.

> ANSWERS
> **1** react   **2** specifically   **3** Furthermore
> **4** eventually   **5** considerable

Unit review

Students work through the list alone to decide what they can and can't do. They discuss their answers in pairs, including what they remember from the unit about each point. Finally, open up the discussion to include the whole class. Pay particular attention to any boxes that the students didn't check. Explore with them ways of overcoming any remaining problems.

Extra research task

As a take-home activity, ask students to research the history of a well-known technology device or invention, such as computers, TVs, the Internet. They should find at least five important dates to add to their timeline, and prepare a short talk detailing these. The research can be presented at the beginning of the next lesson.

5 SUCCESS

LISTENING 1	Listening for vocabulary in context
LISTENING 2	Listening to summarize
STUDY SKILL	Studying for tests
VOCABULARY	Prefixes
GRAMMAR	Quantifiers
SPEAKING	Using discourse markers to compare and contrast

Warm-up

Write the word *success* on the board. Check the meaning with students. Then ask students to close their eyes, and call out words they associate with *success*. These could be synonyms, or examples of success. This is an association exercise, in which students make their own connections. There are no right or wrong answers. Write up the students' words in a "word cloud" on the board. When there are no more words being said, ask students to open their eyes and read the words they have all associated with *success*. This should be a fun, positive way to start the unit.

Discussion point

Ask students to read through the infographic and highlight any words they don't know. Give them time to work in small groups, checking the meaning of these words. Invite whole-class feedback. Ask other students to provide definitions for words which any group doesn't know, and only provide the definition yourself for any words which none of the students know.

Students then discuss the questions with a partner, or in small groups. Monitor and encourage further discussion through the use of follow-up questions (e.g., *Why do you say that? What do you feel about that?*).

Invite whole-class feedback. Establish which three items from the infographic are seen as most important by the class overall. Build a list of different ways to celebrate. Add your own. Then review the list with the class to see how general it is (e.g., *Do we all tend to celebrate in the same way? Does the way we celebrate depend on our age / gender / nationality / background?*).

VIDEO

Before you watch

Focus the students' attention on the photo and the title (*Coding school*). Ask what students know about the topic. They then discuss the questions with a partner. Invite class feedback, adding key words from the video to the board, and checking meaning (e.g., *coding / intensive / graduated / Product Manager / Silicon Valley / merit / traditional schooling / employment / feedback / hiring partners*).

> **POSSIBLE ANSWER**
> **3** *Silicon Valley* is in the state of California, in the U.S.A., and was once home to computer manufacturers, and now the world's largest high-tech companies are based there. *Hiring partner* is a synonym for employer, someone who hires you to do a job.

While you watch

Give students time to read through the sentences. Students discuss the sentences in pairs, checking meaning and predicting the answers. Play the video. Allow students time afterwards to compare their answers with a partner's.

> **ANSWERS**
> **1** F (He studied there two years ago.)   **2** F (The course is ten weeks.)   **3** T   **4** T   **5** T

See page 108 for the video script.

After you watch

Ask students to discuss the questions in pairs, or in small groups. Monitor and encourage extended discussion with follow-up questions. Focus on question 2 during class feedback. List the factors on the board which students suggest as being helpful for success (e.g., *a good education*). Then ask students to consider factors which might make success more difficult. List those in a second column (e.g., *not coming from a wealthy family*). Ask students to review the two lists and Walter's view, and then give a final assessment of whether effort and study are sufficient for success.

LISTENING 1

Skill, effort or luck?

A Vocabulary preview

1 Read out the words in bold. Students work alone to match the words to the definitions. Allow time for students to compare their answers with a partner's before going through the answers with the class.

ANSWERS

1 e   2 h   3 f   4 g   5 a   6 c   7 d   8 b

2 Students complete the sentences with the words in bold from Exercise 1. Go through the answers with the class.

ANSWERS

1 situation   2 Though   3 surprised   4 effort
5 reward   6 admitted   7 load   8 apply

Extension activity

Ask students to write Yes / No questions (e.g., *Have you* **applied** *for a job in the last year?*). Students then either interview one person (with the open-ended questions), or conduct a mini-survey (with the Yes / No questions). Ask students to give feedback to the whole class on the most interesting information they found out.

B Before you listen

Activating prior knowledge

Allow students time to read through the statements, and to consider which of them are true in their opinion. They then discuss their views with a partner. Monitor and encourage further discussion with follow-up questions. Ask students to give feedback on the main points of their discussion to the whole class.

C Global listening

Listening for main ideas

Explain the context of the listening (three students are having an informal discussion). Allow students time to read the question and the information they need to match. Play the audio. Go through the answers with the class.

AUDIO SCRIPT

🎧 **Track 5.1**

JUAN: I sure am glad it's the last day of the semester. What about you, Roberto?

ROBERTO: Me, too, Juan. I had a really busy year. I had a full load of classes, worked part-time at the bookstore, and I got sick. I'm glad this year is ending! Aren't you, Daniel?

DANIEL: I like going to school. I don't want this semester to end!

JUAN: Well, I have to admit that I did not study much at all, but I'm still ready to take some time off. Were you happy with your grades? I was. Even though I didn't study much, I still did OK in the final exams, even in math.

DANIEL: How did you do that?

JUAN: I think I just got lucky. The exams were pretty easy. My brother took the same classes two years ago, so I knew a little about the courses already. I don't think I will be this lucky next time. Besides, my exam grades were good, but not as good as they could have been if I had studied harder. I wish I had put a little effort in to get even better scores.

ROBERTO: I made a big effort to study. It was such a tiring year, but it paid off in the end because I got the grades I wanted. Except in science, but that's a tough subject!

DANIEL: I didn't study as much as you, but I got excellent grades. It sounds surprising, but it makes sense. To be honest, I'm very good at taking exams; I work well under pressure and I can predict the kind of questions they'll ask, so I only study those parts of the subjects. I really enjoyed the exams I took, actually!

ROBERTO: Wow, that's an amazing skill to have, Daniel. Honestly, I feel really relieved. I worked really hard in all of my classes because I needed to do well so that I could apply for admission to university. My goal is to get into medical school one day, so I need good grades. All of my studying paid off.

DANIEL: Great!

JUAN: Congratulations to both of you! I guess it is true what they say, Roberto. Effort equals reward. If you work hard, you are rewarded. You deserve to be noticed for your good work. I'll try to put more effort in next year so that my grades improve.

ROBERTO: Thanks, Juan. What are you guys doing over the summer break?…

ANSWERS

1 b   2 a

D Close listening

Listening for vocabulary in context

Read through the *Listening for vocabulary in context* box with students. Check understanding of *roots*, by writing *successful* and *unsuccessful* on the board. Elicit the root word *success,* and ask what type of word it is (**Answer:** *a noun*). Then ask what the addition of *-ful* and *un-* do (**Answers:** *make the word into an adjective, and make the idea negative*). Read through the rest of the box and encourage students to ask questions to check their understanding.

1 Students listen to the excerpt and complete the paragraphs. Allow students time to check in pairs before playing the audio again. Go through the answers with the class. Ask students to identify any features from the *Close listening* box present for each answer (e.g., *I'm very good at taking exams …, the next part explains what he means by this, so we know the following phrase, with the key word pressure, will be an example of something that helps in exams.*).

AUDIO SCRIPT

🎧 **Track 5.2**

DANIEL: I didn't study as much as you, Roberto, but I got excellent grades. It sounds surprising, but it makes sense. To be honest, I'm very good at taking exams; I work well under pressure and I can predict the kind of questions they'll ask, so I only study those parts of the subjects. I really enjoyed the exams I took, actually!

ROBERTO: Wow, that's an amazing skill to have, Daniel. Honestly, I feel really relieved. I worked really hard in all of my classes because I needed to do well so that I could apply for admission to college. My goal is to get into medical school one day, so I need good grades. All of my studying paid off.

ANSWERS
1 sense   2 pressure   3 subjects   4 skill
5 relieved   6 admission

---

2 Students compare their paragraphs. Have a short discussion on what mistakes they have made.

E Critical thinking

Assessing and evaluating situations and information is a key part of critical thinking. To do this you need to be able to consider the facts in a situation, and weigh them against criteria. Here, students are required to consider the people involved in the discussion and the students' own criteria for giving rewards. They then need to assess whether the people deserve a reward. The second critical thinking skill used is comparison of self to an external situation. Students are required to decide which of the three they are most similar to, and to explain and justify their answers.

Students work alone to consider their own criteria for giving rewards. Ask questions to help them formulate their ideas (e.g., *Does it depend on the amount of effort made? Is only the result in important? Is the result not important?*). Students then discuss the questions in small groups. Each group reports back the main points of their discussion to the class.

STUDY SKILLS ⟩

Studying for tests

Warm-up

Do another association exercise with students (similar to the *Warm-up* exercise at the start of the unit). Write the word *tests* on the board. Ask students to close their eyes, and call out words they associate with tests. Students make their own connections, and there are no right or wrong answers. Write up the students' words in a "word cloud" on the board. When there are no more words being said, ask students to open their eyes, and read the words they have all associated with *tests*. Analyze with students whether the words are positive or negative overall, and elicit why that might be the case.

---

1 Students discuss the questions in pairs. Then put pairs together to form small groups, and ask students to explain the main points of their previous discussion. During whole-class feedback, build a list of materials to use to study for a test on the board, including websites, etc., which other students might find useful.

2 Students discuss the tips in pairs. Ask them to identify the five most important ones in their view. Also, ask the students to categorize the tips in terms of when they should be used (e.g., *Are the tips for the long-term, mid-term, or immediately before the exam?*). Elicit whole-class feedback.

3 Students relate the tips to themselves, identifying which they do, and which they will start doing. They could also review the tips in terms of which they do (or would) find easy, and which would be more challenging for them on a personal level. Share answers as a whole class, and build a list of other tips on the board. Encourage students to take a copy of this for future reference.

What is success?

A Vocabulary preview

1 Ask students to discuss the meaning of the words in the box in pairs. Share ideas as a whole class. Highlight if any of the definitions given are wrong. If the definitions are in the correct area of meaning, indicate this, and tell the students the meaning will be confirmed by completing the exercise. Students work alone to complete the text. Ask students to check in pairs, and then go through the answers with the class.

> ANSWERS
> 1 According to   2 graduate   3 career   4 minimum
> 5 disagree   6 attempted   7 society

2 Students discuss the questions with their partner. Ask each student to report to the class the most interesting thing their partner told them.

Extension activity

Students write two more questions using words from the box in Exercise 1 (e.g., *How many people in your family have graduated?*). They then mingle and ask other students their questions. They should report back the most surprising answer they heard, and also the most common answer.

B Before you listen

Activating prior knowledge

1 Students review the list of achievements and check those they have achieved. Ask them to add up to two more of their own personal achievements to the list. Take a tally as a whole class to see how many students have achieved each thing. Add the list of other student achievements to the board, and see if others have also achieved these.

2 Students read the quote and answer the questions. During whole-class feedback, explore the students' answers to question 2 with follow-up questions (e.g., *Why do you say that?*).

C Global listening

Listening to summarize

With books closed, write the word *summary* on the board. Ask students when they would expect to hear a speaker summarize the main ideas of a talk. When students have given their ideas, ask them to open their books, and read through the *Listening to summarize* box to check. Give further time for students to review the

complete box. Check understanding of *a credit to the source* (i.e., *a reference to where the information is from*).

1 Students listen to *What is success?* and then circle the sentence which best summarizes the information.

AUDIO SCRIPT

 Track 5.3

PRESENTER: You're all here because you want to know how to be successful. I think the first thing we need to do is make sure we all know what success is. Does anyone know? Yes, you have your hand up. What do you think?

AUDIENCE MEMBER 1: Having a lot of money.

AUDIENCE MEMBER 2: A good job.

AUDIENCE MEMBER 3: Finishing college.

PRESENTER: According to the dictionary, success is "the achievement of something that you planned to do, or attempted to do". If that's the case, if you planned or attempted to have a lot of money, then you're successful. If you have the job you planned to have, then you're successful. The key is whether or not it is YOU that planned or YOU that attempted. YOU. Not someone else, YOU. It doesn't matter what society tells us. Success can only be determined by you. Would most of you agree that finishing college is a success? Would most of you agree that Mark Zuckerberg and Bill Gates are successful? Was Steve Jobs successful? I think so, too. But none of them graduated from college. Does this now mean they're not successful?

Bill Gates wanted to start a company, so he attempted it. Therefore, he's a success. Is someone who ran a marathon more successful than someone who didn't run it? No—you can't fail something if that something is not part of your plan. The point is that every person decides what success is for him or herself. Sure, society makes us feel that doctors are more successful than people who choose other career paths, but I disagree. In my opinion, anyone is successful if they're doing what they planned to do. All of your answers: a lot of money, a good job, finishing college: you're all right. But what other answers might we now have?

AUDIENCE MEMBER 4: A happy family?

PRESENTER: Yes!

AUDIENCE MEMBER 5: A nice garden?

PRESENTER: Yes, again! The specifics might be different for everyone. How do you define a lot of money? A CEO wants to buy an expensive car. He needs a lot of money to do it. He works hard, makes enough money, gets a bonus, and buys the car. Success. To a student who works at the fast-food restaurant on the corner for minimum wage, who eventually saves enough money to pay for school. He is successful, too. Many people will say that working hard, practicing, and focusing will help you achieve your goals. Others claim persisting through failure, having passion, and taking small steps pave the way to success. I believe all of those are good things to do. What I want to stress is that the characteristics for achieving success might be the same, but the difference is the end goal. The man who plans to finish college, and does so, is just as successful as the man who plans to run a marathon and does so. The CEO who plans to make a million dollars is just as successful as the man who works hard to earn enough money to pay for his groceries for the month. There is a famous saying that says, "Beauty is in the eye of the beholder." I believe success is the same.

Remember this: If you choose it, you plan it, you attempt it, then you succeed.

ANSWER
b

---

2 Give students time to review the list of main points. They discuss which are appropriate for inclusion in a summary of the talk with a partner. Go through the answers with the class. Highlight the difference in length and focus of the two summaries, and remind students of the main point of a summary, as outlined in the skills box.

ANSWERS
2, 3, 5, 8, 9

---

3 Students review both summaries and, based on their answers to Exercise 2, choose the best one. They then compare their choice with a partner's, and explain their reasons.

ANSWER
3 B
POSSIBLE ANSWER
It is direct and includes the main ideas, without extra details or examples.

D Close listening
Listening for details

Allow time for students to read through the statements. Then play the audio again. Students decide which statements are *T* (True) or *F* (False). Give time for students to compare answers in pairs. Play the audio again if needed. Go through the answers with the class.

AUDIO SCRIPT
 Track 5.3

ANSWERS
1 F (Success is the achievement of something that you planned to do, or attempted to do.)
2 T
3 F (Bill Gates wanted to start a company.)
4 F (Anyone is successful if they're doing what they planned to do.)
5 T
6 F ("Beauty is in the eye of the beholder".)

E Critical thinking

In critical thinking, it is important to be able to support and justify an opinion. If time for research is available, then facts and statistics can be used. However, if there is no time for formal research, then justifications for opinions should be given with reasoned and logical arguments, along with examples from personal experience.

Give students time to review the questions alone, and make a note of their ideas. Then ask them to discuss their views in small groups. During whole-class feedback, ask if anyone has changed their view in the light of the discussion.

PRONUNCIATION

Pronunciation for listening
Homophones

With books closed, write the following sentences on the board: *We have ___ hands. We use them ___ eat. We use them to write ___* Elicit the missing words (**Answer:** *two / to / too*). Ask students what is special about these words (**Answer:** *they sound the same but have different meanings*), and if they know the name of them. Ask students to open their books, and read through the *Homophones* box to check their ideas.

1 Highlight the point in the skills box about using the sentence context to decide which word was heard. Quickly check the meaning of each of the words in Exercise 1 with students. Then play the audio, and students circle the words they hear. Allow time for students to check their answers in pairs, before playing the audio again. Go through the answers with the class.

ANSWERS
1 blew 2 night 3 do 4 seems 5 whether

2 Students choose one of the words in each pair and write a sentence that includes it. Monitor the activity, and check that the meaning is clear from the context of the students' sentences.

3 Students read out their sentences for their partner to decide which word is used.

VOCABULARY

Vocabulary development
Prefixes

With books closed, write *disagree, inconvenient, impossible, return,* and *overachiever* on the board. Ask students to identify the connection between the words. Field their answers, and if they do not spot the prefixes, erase *dis* from *disagree*. Continue to do this until the students recognize the prefixes. Add the prefixes back to the words if erased, and then ask for suggestions as to what each prefix might mean. Then ask students to open their books, and check their ideas by reading through the *Prefixes* box.

1 Students work alone to complete the chart. Students then compare their answers with a partner's. Ask students to come to the board to complete the chart you have copied there. Review the chart as a whole class, confirming or correcting as appropriate.

ANSWERS
1 disappear—go away 2 inconsistent—not the same
3 dislike—not like 4 incomplete—not finished
5 impatient—not wanting to wait 6 rewrite—written again 7 overcautious—more careful than necessary
8 rearrange—put into a different order

2 Students complete the questions with words from Exercise 1.

ANSWERS
1 disappear 2 dislike 3 incomplete 4 impatient
5 rearrange 6 rewrite 7 inconsistent
(Item 7 [overcautious] isn't used.)

3 Students ask and answer the questions. Ask them to report back on two questions they had the most different answers on.

VOCABULARY

Academic words

1 Before looking at the definitions, ask students to work in pairs to read the sentences and discuss the meaning of the words in bold. When finished, students work alone to match the words to the definitions below them. Ask students to check their answers in pairs, and then go through the answers with the class.

ANSWERS
1 g 2 e 3 b 4 d 5 c 6 h 7 a 8 f

2 Students ask and answer the questions in pairs.

Extension activity

Students work in pairs to create their own mini-tests to give to another pair. They choose eight words from the *Vocabulary development* and *Academic words* sections. They write fill-in-the-blank sentences for the words, and place all the options in a box above the sentences. Monitor and check the sentences as they do this. When students have finished, pairs swap papers and complete the mini-tests. If the answers are written on separate sheets of paper, the tests can be swapped several times.

SPEAKING

Speaking model

Write *a lot of* and *unlike* on the board. Then ask students to open their books and read through the aims for the *Speaking* section. Ask students to match the technical terms "*quantifiers*" and "*discourse markers*" to the words on the board. Some students are less comfortable with technical terms and benefit from immediately understanding what they mean by seeing actual examples. Remind students that all language and skills in the unit build towards the success of the final speaking task.

A Model

Show or reproduce the charts on the board at the front of the class if possible. Focus the students on the charts, and ask questions to check understanding (**Possible answers:** *What is compared, periods of time or different countries? different countries; How many options were given to the respondents? Three*). Then ask students to work together to identify the significant differences (**Possible answers:** *Many more young people in the U.K. think luck is most important. Many fewer in the U.K. think education is important*). Ask for suggestions as a whole class. Students then read the model and answer the questions.

B Discuss

Students discuss the questions in small groups. Monitor and encourage further discussion. Ask groups to report back on one or two key points from their discussion.

Extension activity

Conduct a whole-class survey and produce a pie chart to show the results from the class. This can then be compared to the charts in the model. Elicit from students the question for the survey (**Possible answer:** *Which is more important for getting a job: education, work experience, or luck?*). Collect the results, and if possible, have a student record the results in a data spreadsheet. Generate and display a chart.

GRAMMAR

Quantifiers

Warm-up

With books closed, write *More* and *Less* on the board at the head of two columns. Then write up in a jumbled order, or display on large cards, the following quantifiers: *a lot of, significantly, considerably, most, a little, slightly, marginally, least, a few of.* Ask students to discuss in pairs which quantifiers indicate *more* and which indicate *less.* They should come to the board to write the word, or place the card in the correct place. When completed, ask students to open their books, read the *Quantifiers* box and check.

1   Students work alone to choose the correct quantifier for each sentence. Allow time for students to compare their answers in pairs before going through the answers with the class.

ANSWERS
1 significantly   2 most   3 A few   4 marginal
5 considerably   6 most

2   Students discuss the possibilities in pairs. Go through the answers as a class.

POSSIBLE ANSWERS
1 Most   2 a lot of   3 marginally   4 a little
5 considerably   6 a little

SPEAKING

Speaking skill
Using discourse markers to compare and contrast

1   Read through the *Using discourse markers to compare and contrast* box with students. Then ask them to complete the table with the phrases from the box. Go through answers with the class. Then give students a few minutes to study the chart. After two minutes, ask students to close their books and build up the chart on the board. If students cannot remember a phrase, provide the first letter, and add to this until they recall it.

ANSWERS
Compare: *as … as, in the same way, like, likewise, similarly, the same as*
Contrast: *conversely, in contrast, on the contrary, unlike*

2   Students work alone to identify whether the sentences are comparing or contrasting, and then choose the correct word accordingly. Ask students to check in pairs, and then check as a class.

ANSWERS
1 However   2 In contrast   3 the same   4 unlike
5 however   6 Conversely

PRONUNCIATION

Pronunciation for speaking
Stress in modifiers before data

Read the *Stress in modifiers before data* box with the students. Model the language, placing emphasis on the modifiers before the data. Highlight that the stress indicates the speaker's attitude to the data. Give students time to experiment with saying the example sentences from the skills box in pairs. Monitor and help as needed.

1 Students listen and complete the sentences with the correct modifier. If the class needs more support, write the modifiers on the board in a jumbled order. Go through the answers with the class.

AUDIO SCRIPT

🎧 **Track 5.5**

1 There was a staggering difference in the number of students that enrolled in the class in 2017 compared to 2018.

2 The data showed a remarkable number of students feel pressured to do well in exams.

3 Only 3% of interviewees said that they would like to do sports in their free time.

4 As much as 90% of respondents agreed that they would like the university to open a new science block.

5 A huge 98% of interviewees felt skill was very important in exam performance.

6 An impressive 56% of respondents actually said they would like to take a different course next year.

ANSWERS
1 staggering 2 remarkable 3 Only 4 As much as
5 huge 6 impressive

---

2 Students practice saying the sentences in Exercise 1 with a partner. Monitor and assist as necessary, praising appropriate and effective use of emphasis.

SPEAKING

Speaking task
Brainstorm and plan

Read through the task with students. Remind them that the language they have studied in this unit supports this final task. Give students time to look back quickly through the unit as a reminder of the content.

Students work in small groups to analyze the data. They should note points that can be compared or contrasted. They should also identify words and phrases they can use in their presentations. For this, encourage students to complete a more thorough review of the unit, noting useful language and vocabulary.

Students work through the three planning stages together. First, they decide on the structure of the talk. Then they identify specific quantifiers and discourse markers for key points in the presentation. Finally, they decide how to summarize the key points. Highlight the *Useful language* box, and encourage students to incorporate it into their presentations.

Speak and share

Students work in new groups, and each student gives their individual presentations. Monitor and take notes on effective language use, focusing on the target language of the unit. Also make a note of language points which could be improved by using more of the target language.

Once all the presentations are complete, students return to their original groups to report on the experience. They should share their views on what they feel went well and why. Then bring the class together and provide feedback on language use. Highlight effective language use, and encourage peer correction of errors.

Reflect

Students reflect on the questions alone. Ask them to make a note of their reflections, and review them next time they need to give a presentation.

REVIEW

Wordlist

Students work in pairs or small groups to work through the *Wordlist*, checking that they all remember what each word or phrase means, how to pronounce it, and how it was used in the unit. Go through the list carefully with the class.

Academic words review

Students work through the sentences, check their answers in pairs, and then give feedback to the class.

ANSWERS
1 illustrate 2 author 3 invest 4 define
5 immigration

Unit review

Students work through the list alone to decide what they can and can't do. They discuss their answers in pairs, including what they remember from the unit about each point. Finally, open up the discussion to include the whole class. Pay particular attention to any boxes that the students didn't check. Explore with them ways of overcoming any remaining problems.

Extra research task

As a take-home activity, ask students to research a "successful" person. They should identify what area the person is successful in, what were the challenges, and what advice, if any, the person gives. The research can be presented in a series of mini-talks at the start of the next lesson.

---

6 PRESSURE

LISTENING 1	Listening for how opinions are supported
LISTENING 2	Listening for cause and effect
STUDY SKILL	Enabling good discussion
VOCABULARY	Collocations: Expressions with *get*
GRAMMAR	Giving advice using modals in conditional sentences
SPEAKING	Explaining something you don't know the word for

Warm-up

Play a mime game. Mime *listening to music* (e.g., *Put hands to ears as if you are wearing headphones*). Elicit *listen(ing) to music,* and write it on the board. Mime the other five actions from the infographic, elicit or provide the phrases, and write them on the board. Ask the students what the actions help us to do (**Possible answer:** *relax / feel less stressed*). Ask for a few more suggestions of things to do to relax (the actions should be possible to be mimed), and add them to the board. Students work in pairs: Student A sits with their back to the board, so the phrases cannot be seen. Student B mimes an action, and Student A guesses the action. Set a time limit, and tell students to start. When the time is finished, award one point for each correct phrase. Students then change roles.

Discussion point

Give students time to read through the infographic. They then discuss the questions with a partner. Ask students to then share their answers with a new pair. Together, they should draw up a list of four other sources of stress (for question 2), and tips to deal with these (for question 3). Share answers as a whole class.

Extension activity

Students write posters for their tips for stress management and display these on the walls of the classroom, as a positive influence for the rest of the term.

VIDEO

Before you watch

Draw a flower on the board, elicit the word *flower,* and ask the students what people do with them (**Possible answers:** *grow, pick, sell, buy, eat, paint, arrange*). Write the answers on the board, making sure to include *arrange,* and check the meaning of this word.

Establish how to pronounce each number in the box. Students then work in pairs to predict which numbers complete each sentence.

While you watch

1 Play the video. Students watch, and then review their answers with their partner. Go through the answers with the class.

ANSWERS		
1 15	**2** 20	**3** 500

2 Give students time to read through the text, and check any vocabulary as necessary. Students can discuss, and try to recall their answers with a partner. They then watch again to check.

ANSWERS
1 Tokyo **2** choosing flowers in a shop
3 men **4** it relaxes them

See page 109 for the video script.

After you watch

Students discuss the questions in pairs or small groups. Monitor and encourage students to use follow-up questions to extend the discussion. Go through the answers with the class.

LISTENING 1

Peer pressure

A Vocabulary preview

1 Students work alone to match the words in bold to the definitions. Ask students to check in pairs, and then check as a class.

ANSWERS
1 h **2** b **3** c **4** a **5** e **6** g **7** f **8** d

2 Students work alone to complete the sentences with the words from Exercise 1. Go through the answers with the class.

3 Students review sentences 1–6 alone to decide if they agree or disagree with them. Encourage students to make notes of key ideas to support their views. Then students share their views with a partner's. Students then look at sentences 7–8 in pairs, and where they can, describe the situation. During whole-class feedback, ask pairs to report on one sentence they didn't agree on, and the situations they talked about.

B Before you listen

Activating prior knowledge

With books closed, write *Peer pressure* on the board. Remind students that *peer* was in the *Vocabulary* section (and *pressure* is the title of the unit). Ask for student suggestions about the meaning of the phrase. Write key words and phrases they give on the board. Students then open their books and read the definition to check their ideas.

With a partner, students read through the five situations, and decide if they are examples of peer pressure. Ask students to explain their answers in whole-class feedback.

ANSWERS
1 4 5

C Global listening

Listening for main ideas

Refer students to the *Glossary*. Ask them which word it contains from the *Vocabulary* section (**Answer:** *direct*), and what has changed the word (**Answer:** *The use of the prefix "in," to make the word have the opposite meaning*).

Tell students they are going to listen to a discussion between two students about peer pressure. Allow time for students to review the list of topics, and check the meaning of vocabulary as necessary. Highlight that one of the topics is not discussed. Play the audio, and allow students to compare answers after listening.

AUDIO SCRIPT

 Track 6.1

LAILA: OK Susan, let's look at question one. What is peer pressure?

SUSAN: Let's see … I think peer pressure is … the pressure you get from your friends. For example, my friends sometimes try and get me to do things I shouldn't.

LAILA: But it's not just pressure from friends, but from anyone your own age. Those are your peers. So, peer pressure is from people your own age.

SUSAN: Right.

LAILA: OK, so question 2. When do most peer pressure situations occur?

SUSAN: Um, I think … most peer pressure situations occur … at school. This is because at school you're with your peers all day. You have to deal with lots of different types of people.

LAILA: I think it's after school.

SUSAN: Really?

LAILA: Yeah. I think there is a lot of pressure to get the right kind of job once you leave school and to buy your own house.

SUSAN: Interesting … OK, I'm happy to revise my answer to that. OK, so next question, which I think relates to that. Which type is worse, direct pressure or pressure that is indirect?

LAILA: What's the difference?

SUSAN: Direct pressure is when a person asks you to do something. The person says things that push you toward a certain choice.

LAILA: Uh, Susan, I'm not sure I understand.

SUSAN: Think of it this way. Someone says they won't be friends with you if you don't do something. Another instance would be when someone calls you a name to make you feel bad.

LAILA: Uh, I see. So when the pressure is indirect, it means nothing is actually said to you. So, when you see others doing something, you feel pressure to do the same? Like when your friends all get a job, you feel like you should get a job?

SUSAN: Exactly, or like when a group stands apart from others and talks and laughs. They don't include you and you feel left out. Or when they think they're really cool and look at you like you're not.

LAILA: So … which is worse?

SUSAN: Direct pressure is definitely worse.

LAILA: Why is that?

SUSAN: It's just terrible when your peers don't include you. Don't you agree?

LAILA: Um, let me think …. No, I don't think direct pressure is so bad. Indirect pressure seems worse.

SUSAN: Why is that?

LAILA: Well, I think it's easier to deal with direct pressure, and be … you know … I can't think of the exact word. It's, uh, similar to "reasonable."

SUSAN: You mean logical?

LAILA: Yeah, in my opinion it's easy to be logical with people. Let me just add that I have some experience with people like that.

SUSAN: I don't see it that way at all.

LAILA: Let's go onto the next question.

SUSAN: OK. What's the best way to avoid peer pressure?

LAILA: I think the best way is to make friends with people who behave like you. The reason for this is you'll be less likely to get in trouble.

SUSAN: That's a good idea, but I think the best thing to do, if you're pressured to do something you don't want to do, is to walk away. If you do this, they'll easily get the message.

LAILA: Um, maybe … Oh, this question is interesting. Who is the best person to talk to if you feel peer pressure?

SUSAN: Um … I suppose … a teacher.

LAILA: Well, I think the best person to talk to is a parent. If your parents know about the pressure, they'll get behind you.

SUSAN: Imagine someone is pressuring you to do something you know is wrong. What would your parents do if you told them?

LAILA: They'd support me. They wouldn't get angry or upset. They'd be happy I told them.

SUSAN: OK, so, last question. Can peer pressure be a positive thing?

LAILA: In my opinion … no.

SUSAN: I think it definitely can.

LAILA: I can't see how.

SUSAN: Let me explain. If my friends get good grades, I'll try and do the same. I'll want to do the same thing as my friends.

LAILA: Yeah, I see what you mean.

ANSWERS

1 b **2** f **3** a **4** e **5** g **6** c (d is not mentioned.)

D Close listening

Listening for how opinions are supported

1 Before reading the *Listening for how opinions are supported* box, students listen to the whole discussion again to identify who gives each opinion. Before playing the audio, allow students time to read through the opinions. After listening, students compare their answers in pairs. Go through the answers with the class.

AUDIO SCRIPT

 Track 6.1

ANSWERS

1 S **2** S **3** L **4** L **5** S

Read through the skills box with students. Give them a short time to study the three categories and the phrases. Then with books closed, elicit the three categories (**Answers:** *Giving an example; Explaining further; Giving a reason*). Write these on the board. Then, ask the students to recall the phrases from the box and add them to the board.

2 Students listen and match the signposts to the rest of the excerpt. Go through the answers with the class.

AUDIO SCRIPT

 Track 6.2

1

LAILA: OK Susan, let's look at question one. What is peer pressure?

SUSAN: Let's see … I think peer pressure is … the pressure you get from your friends. For example, my friends sometimes try and get me to do things I shouldn't.

LAILA: But it's not just pressure from friends, but from anyone your own age. Those are your peers. So, peer pressure is from people your own age.

2

LAILA: OK, so question 2. When do most peer pressure situations occur?

SUSAN: Um, I think … most peer pressure situations occur … at school. This is because at school you're with your peers all day. You have to deal with lots of different types of people.

LAILA: I think it's after school.

3

LAILA: Well, I think it's easier to deal with direct pressure, and be … you know … I can't think of the exact word. It's, uh, similar to "reasonable."

SUSAN: You mean logical?

LAILA: Yeah, in my opinion it's easy to be logical with people. Let me just add that I have some experience with people like that.

SUSAN: I don't see it that way at all.

4

SUSAN: OK. What's the best way to avoid peer pressure?

LAILA: I think the best way is to make friends with people who behave like you. The reason for this is you'll be less likely to get in trouble.

SUSAN: That's a good idea, but I think the best thing to do, if you're pressured to do something you don't want to do, is to walk away. If you do this, they'll easily get the message.

5

SUSAN: OK, so last question. Can peer pressure be a positive thing?

LAILA: In my opinion ... no.

SUSAN: I think it definitely can.

LAILA: I can't see how.

SUSAN: Let me explain. If my friends get good grades, I'll try and do the same. I'll want to do the same thing as my friends.

ANSWERS
1 d **2** a **3** c **4** e **5** b

E Critical thinking

Students work in groups to analyze their own context in relation to the broader problem of peer pressure. Monitor and encourage students to support their opinions using the signpost phrases from the *Close listening* section.

Ask students to recall the examples of positive peer pressure from the *Listening* section (**Answers:** *in Before you listen, a study group getting good grades asks you to join; discussion between Laila and Susan about the influence of friends getting good grades*). Students then discuss examples of positive peer pressure, and their own experience with it.

PRONUNCIATION

Pronunciation for listening
Taking time to think

Allow time for students to read through the information. Ask them what phrases people use in their own language while they are thinking, and what types of fillers are used.

---

1 Read through the task with students. Highlight that they should check a box in one of the two columns for each speaker. Play the audio.

AUDIO SCRIPT

🎧 **Track 6.3**

1 Listening to music is, you know, um, a great way to relax.

2 Many students try to find creative ways to deal with exam stress.

3 Peer pressure is, uh, something many students have to deal with.

4 There is a TV show on teen pressure at ... let's see ... 10:00 p.m.

5 Doing things like exercising with friends is a good example of positive peer pressure.

6 I wonder why so many people worry about what others think.

ANSWERS
1 Takes time to think **2** Doesn't take time to think
3 Takes time to think **4** Takes time to think
5 Doesn't take time to think **6** Doesn't take time to think

---

2 Focus students' attention on the first sentence, and highlight that an oblique (/) indicates where the speaker pauses. Assign the task and then play the audio. Allow time for students to compare their answers in pairs, and then play the audio again as necessary.

AUDIO SCRIPT

🎧 **Track 6.4**

1 Let's see. I think peer pressure is the pressure you get from your friends.

2 Um, I think most peer pressure situations occur at school.

3 I think it's after school.

4 So, which is worse?

5 Um, I suppose a teacher.

6 In my opinion, no.

ANSWERS
1 Let's see. / I think peer pressure / is the pressure you get from your friends.
2 Um, / I think / most peer pressure situations / occur at school.
3 I think / it's after school.
4 So, / which is worse?
5 Um, / I suppose a teacher.
6 In my opinion, / no.

---

3 Allow time for students to review the task and the excerpts. Then play the audio. Play again as necessary, and go through the answers with the class.

AUDIO SCRIPT

 Track 6.5

SUSAN: It's just terrible when your peers don't include you. Don't you agree?

LAILA: Um, let me think. … No, I don't think direct pressure is so bad. Indirect pressure seems worse.

SUSAN: Why is that?

LAILA: Well, I think it's easier to deal with direct pressure, and be … you know … I can't think of the exact word. It's, uh, similar to "reasonable".

ANSWERS
1 Um, let me think … **2** Well, … **3** you know …
4 uh, …

LISTENING 2 ▶

Exam pressure
A Vocabulary preview

1 Students work alone to review the sentences and match the words in bold to the definitions. Students compare their answers in pairs, and then check as a class.

ANSWERS
1 disappoint **2** reduce **3** compete **4** psychological
5 outline **6** expectations **7** distract **8** demands

---

2 Students review the sentences and decide which are true for them. They then share and discuss their answers with a partner. During whole-class feedback, ask pairs to report back the most interesting facts they found out about each other.

B Before you listen
Activating prior knowledge

1 Review the scale with students and ask them to identify where they are on the line. Draw the scale on the board, and ask students to come to the board to mark where they are. Review the stress levels of the class as a whole. Ask a few students, including some of the least stressed, to explain their position.

---

2 Students work in small groups to discuss the questions. Ask them to report back on who they were most similar to, and most different from in their group.

C Global listening
Listening for main ideas

Give students time to review the task and the topics. Then play the audio. Go through the answers with the class.

AUDIO SCRIPT

 Track 6.6

Good morning. Welcome back to Modern Psychology. Please take your seats, so we can get started.

Today I'm going to talk about a topic I think many of you have experienced—exam pressure. How many of you have experienced exam pressure? … I thought so. Many college students experience some sort of stress. According to a recent survey in the United States, 20% of students said they feel stressed most of the time. Forty percent said they often feel stressed. A quarter of students experience stress every day. And it doesn't matter the sex of the person—males and females both experience exam stress. Many have financial worries, such as college fees, or worry about making new friends, or fitting in. But academic pressure, or to be more specific, the pressure to do well in exams, is what's worrying parents and teachers more and more. So, let's look at some of the causes of exam pressure.

One of the biggest factors causing exam pressure is the lack of preparation for an exam. The more prepared you are for an exam, the more confident—and less stressed—you will likely be. But students have many demands on their time— jobs, other classes, friends. What many students do is study as much as possible just before an exam. In other words, they cram, which just adds to the pressure.

Another factor is the pressure students feel from their parents. Most parents have high expectations of their children and children don't want to disappoint them. Exam pressure can also come from a student's peers. During exams, students compete for high grades.

Other people in the exam can also add stress. Other students may make noise, and even cheat. Teachers or others in the room might distract test-takers by making noise. The temperature may be too high or too low. The lighting may be poor. The desk or chair may be uncomfortable.

When the test is scheduled can also be a factor. There may be too many tests at the same time, like when students have mid-terms or finals.

Finally, the test itself can cause stress. A test that has difficult or unknown content, surprise questions, or tricky instructions can all contribute to exam pressure.

What effect does all this have on the test-taker? For many, the effects aren't so serious. They may feel anxious during a test, but they continue to perform well. For others, the effects are more serious. A person may feel pressure during an exam. As a result, this person may get a headache, feel sick to their stomach, have difficulty breathing, or have an increased heartbeat. They may not get enough sleep and develop poor, or dangerous eating habits because of the pressure. But it's not just physical effects; it's also psychological. A student may develop feelings of anger or depression. They may feel hopeless and lost. They can easily develop a low sense of self-esteem. A lack of motivation to even continue with their studies is often due to the pressures of exams. And, of course, exam pressure can result in the disappointment of parents. This then just adds to the pressure.

How can students deal with the pressure? Many experts agree there are steps to take to reduce the pressure. For example, if you are well prepared for an exam, you shouldn't feel much pressure during the exam. So, develop good study habits, and don't wait until the last minute to prepare for exams. And while good study habits are important, so are good test-taking habits. Do things like read directions carefully, answer questions you know first, and outline an essay before writing. These help save time and give you confidence.

You could try relaxation techniques. You could try breathing slower and deeper during an exam. Or you might close your eyes and relax your body before you start the exam. If nothing works, you could try talking to another person—a friend, a teacher, or a counselor—to get advice on how best to deal with the pressures you face. But remember, it's normal to be a little nervous about an exam. And a little stress can be a good thing—it may help you perform better. It's when the pressure becomes a problem that you may need to get help.

ANSWERS
1, 3, 5, 6

D Close listening

Listening for cause and effect

With books closed, write on the board: *She felt very stressed because of the exam.* Ask *Why did she feel stressed?* (**Answer:** *She had an exam.*) Then ask what was the cause of the stress (**Answer:** the exam), and *What was the result of having an exam?* (**Answer:** *stress*). Then write ***cause*** = exam, ***result*** = stress.

Open books and read through the *Listening for cause and effect* box together. Then ask students to reformulate the sentence on the board using the connecting words and phrases from the skills box (**Possible answers:** *The exam was the reason for her stress. / She felt stressed as a result of the exam.*).

1   With books closed, ask students which causes of exam pressure they remember being mentioned in the lecture. Then open books, and give students time to review the causes of exam pressure. Play the excerpt. Give students time to compare their answers in pairs. Play the audio again as needed for your class.

AUDIO SCRIPT

🎧 **Track 6.7**

One of the biggest factors causing exam pressure is the lack of preparation for an exam. The more prepared you are for an exam the more confident—and less stressed—you will likely be. But students have many demands on their time— jobs, other classes, friends. What many students do is study as much as possible just before an exam. In other words, they cram, which just adds to the pressure.

Another factor is the pressure students feel from their parents. Most parents have high expectations of their children and children don't want to disappoint them. Exam pressure can also come from a student's peers. During exams, students compete for high grades.

Other people in the exam can also add stress. Other students may make noise and even cheat. Teachers or others in the room might distract test-takers by making noise. The temperature may be too high or too low. The lighting may be poor. The desk or chair may be uncomfortable.

When the test is scheduled can also be a factor. There may be too many tests at the same time, like when students have mid-terms or finals.

Finally, the test itself can cause stress. A test that has difficult, or unknown content, surprise questions, or tricky instructions can all contribute to exam pressure.

2 Read through the words in the box with the students, checking meaning and modeling the pronunciation. Students mark the stress on the words and phrases. Then give students time to review the information to be completed. Play the audio, and then go through the answers with the class.

AUDIO SCRIPT

 Track 6.8

What effect does all this have on the test-taker? For many, the effects aren't so serious. They may feel anxious during a test, but they continue to perform well. For others, the effects are more serious. A person may feel pressure during an exam. As a result, this person may get a headache, feel sick to their stomach, have difficulty breathing, or have an increased heartbeat. They may not get enough sleep and develop poor, or dangerous eating habits because of the pressure. But it's not just physical effects; it's also psychological. A student may develop feelings of anger or depression. They may feel hopeless and lost. They can easily develop a low sense of self-esteem. A lack of motivation to even continue with their studies is often due to the pressures of exams. And, of course, exam pressure can result in the disappointment of parents. This then just adds to the pressure.

E Critical thinking

Comparing and contrasting issues is an important aspect of critical thinking. Question 1 gives students the opportunity to identify the similarities and differences of exam stress and peer pressure. Remind students to also consider the positives of exam stress, just as they explored the positive effects of peer pressure in the previous listening section.

In groups, students review the causes and effects of exam pressure, as identified in the lecture. They discuss their opinions of these, focusing on whether they believe there is a strong cause-effect relationship. They then add more to the list. Go through the answers with the class.

STUDY SKILLS

Enabling good discussion

Warm-up

Build a mind map with the class. With books closed, write *Group discussions* in the center of the board. Circle the phrase and then draw lines coming from the phrase leading to the three different labels *What happens?*, *Advantages?*, and *Possible problems?*. Then elicit student ideas for each label, and build the mind map. Alternatively, students could work in small groups to work on the mind map, and then share ideas as a whole class. (**Possible answers:** *What happens? Several people / share ideas / make decisions; Advantages? Hear everyone's opinion / equal roles / effective use of time; Possible problems? People don't listen / someone talks too much / someone doesn't talk / someone is rude / loses focus.*)

With books closed, ask students to work in pairs to discuss how they can get the most out of a discussion. Students should identify useful things to do *before*, *during,* and *after* the discussion. Monitor and encourage discussion about why it is good to do these things. Then ask students to open their books, and ask students to read through the *Enabling good discussion* box to check which of their ideas are included.

1 Students work in pairs to discuss the function of each of the quotes. Go through the answers with the class.

Extension activity

Students work in pairs to identify what could happen if the tips from the *Study skills* box are not followed (**Possible answer:** *If you don't listen to other students, they could feel bad, or try to interrupt you.*).

2 Students review and then answer the question in groups. Monitor the discussion to ensure students are using skills and tips learned on the page.

VOCABULARY

Vocabulary development
Collocations with *get*

Remind students what a collocation is (i.e., *a word or phrase that is often used with another word or phrase*), and give some examples, such as *go away, do business, take a break,* and *get a job.* Ask students to open their books, and read through the *Collocations with get* box with the class.

1. Students work alone to complete the sentences with a *get* collocation from the box. Allow time for students to check in pairs, before going through the answers with the class.

ANSWERS
1 started 2 nowhere 3 the message 4 good grades
5 in touch 6 behind someone 7 going 8 in trouble

2. Students identify the correct collocation with *get* for each sentence. Ask students to check in pairs, and then check as class.

ANSWERS
1 get in touch 2 get started 3 get in trouble
4 get the message 5 get good grades 6 get behind
7 get going 8 get nowhere

VOCABULARY

Academic words

1. Students work alone to match the words in bold to the definitions. Allow time for students to compare their answers in pairs. Go through the answers with the class.

ANSWERS
1 g 2 f 3 e 4 a 5 d 6 h 7 c 8 b

2. Students work alone to complete the sentences with words from Exercise 1. Go through the answers with the class.

ANSWERS
1 depression 2 instance 3 psychology 4 revise
5 occur 6 specific 7 factor 8 sex

3. Allow time for students to review the statements in Exercise 2. Ask them to identify three they agree with the most. They then share and discuss their views of these statements with a partner.

SPEAKING

Speaking model

Read through the aims for the *Speaking* section with the students. Highlight briefly that conditional sentences contain *if*, and give an example of a word ending with a consonant sound (e.g., *work*), so that students understand the technical terms in the aims.

A Analyze

1. Give students time to read through the model, and add the sentences to the correct place in the discussion.

ANSWERS
1 d 2 a 3 b 4 c

2. Students work in pairs to analyze the cause and effects of pressure, as identified in the discussion. Go through the answers with the class.

ANSWERS
Omar: cause—doesn't want to disappoint parents
effect—eats too much junk food, little exercise
Yuki: cause—doesn't have time to prepare for exams
effect—doesn't get good grades
Sara: cause—feels like she doesn't have enough money
effect—stays home all the time

B Discuss

Students discuss the questions in pairs. Monitor and encourage discussion with follow-up questions (e.g., *Why do you say that? What do you think the response would be?*). Go through the answers with the class. List the main points of the advice students give for question 2. Then ask pairs to review the list of advice, and identify the most useful advice in their opinion.

GRAMMAR

Giving advice using modals in conditional sentences

With books closed, write *If you have an exam tomorrow, …* on the board, and ask for suggestions from the class as to how to finish the sentence. Reformulate the language as necessary, and write about some of the suggestions to make complete *present real conditional* sentences. Then write *If I had an exam tomorrow, …*, and ask for suggestions as to how to finish the sentence. The students may have more difficulty with the grammar of this *present unreal conditional* sentence. Underline *had* and ask *Do I have an exam tomorrow?* (**Answer:** *No*). Ask *Is this a real condition?* (**Answer:** *No*). Give an example answer if necessary and highlight the grammar (**Possible answer:** *… I would go to sleep early tonight.*). Highlight the note describing where the comma is placed in the sentence.

Students open their books and read through the *Giving advice using modals in conditional sentences* box. Encourage them to ask a partner questions to check understanding, and then to ask you further questions as necessary.

1   Students work alone to write the sentences. Ask students to check in pairs, and then check as a class.

> **ANSWERS**
> 1 If you don't understand the directions, you should ask the teacher.
> 2 If you feel anxious during an exam, you might try breathing deeply.
> 3 If you don't have enough time, you should answer the easy questions.
> 4 If you miss the exam, you could ask to take it later.
> 5 If you are well-prepared, you shouldn't have any problems.
> 6 If you don't have good test-taking skills, you might consider taking a class.

2   Review the second half of the skills box. Then students write advice beginning with *If I were you, …* Go through their ideas with the class.

SPEAKING

Speaking skill
Explaining something you don't know the word for

With books closed, use phrases from the *Explaining something you don't know the word for* box to describe *peer pressure*, without saying the actual phrase. Encourage students to guess what you are trying to say. Then elicit what the problem was (i.e., *that you did not know the actual phrase*). Students then open their books and read through the skills box.

1   Students work alone to match the sentences to the words or phrases they describe. Allow time for students to compare their answers with a partner's, before going through the answers with the class.

> **ANSWERS**
> 1 c 2 f 3 e 4 d 5 b 6 a

2   Students work in pairs to complete the conversations with words from the unit. Go through the answers with the class.

> **ANSWERS**
> 1 anxious 2 peer 3 in touch 4 direct
> 5 get going 6 compete

3   Allow time for students to review the skills box and Exercises 1 and 2. Ask them to underline the useful expressions for explaining something when they don't know the word for it. Then put students into small groups, and ask them to take turns explaining the words in the box.

PRONUNCIATION

Pronunciation for speaking
Consonant sounds at word boundaries

Read through the *Consonant sounds at word boundaries* box with students, modeling and drilling the example language.

1   Give students time to review the conversation. Ask them to identify where they think they will hear examples of linked words (catenation). Then play the audio while students circle the places. Allow time for students to compare their answers in pairs. Play the audio again, then check the answers with the class.

AUDIO SCRIPT

🎧 **Track 6.9**

SHIRA: Anna, we can't go to the library today as it's closed.

ANNA: Oh no, I wanted to get some books. I have an exam Monday, and I really need to study. Do you know when it reopens?

SHIRA: I think it's open again tomorrow. You could try the library on the other side of town if you need the books today.

ANNA: Good idea! Do you want to come with me?

SHIRA: Yes, I'll be ready in an hour. I need to drop off some books. My exams finished yesterday.

ANNA: Oh wow, lucky you. I still have three more to take.

ANSWERS

SHIRA: Anna, we can't go to the library today as it's closed.

ANNA: Oh no, I wanted to get some books. I have an exam Monday, and I really need to study. Do you know when it reopens?

SHIRA: I think it's open again tomorrow. You could try the library on the other side of town if you need the books today.

ANNA: Good idea! Do you want to come with me?

SHIRA: Yes, I'll be ready in an hour. I need to drop off some books. My exams finished yesterday.

ANNA: Oh wow, lucky you. I still have three more to take.

2 Play the audio again while students cross out the consonants that are not pronounced. Allow time for students to compare their answers in pairs. Play the audio again, pausing after each instance for students to check their answers.

3 Students practice the conversation in pairs. Monitor, assist, and encourage as appropriate.

SPEAKING

Speaking task
Brainstorm and plan

Students work alone to complete the chart with their opinion on each idea for reducing stress. They should make a note of supporting ideas as they do this, particularly for those ideas they identify as *great* or *terrible*.

Students then discuss the chart with a partner, supporting their views with the ideas they noted earlier. If necessary, they can make adjustments to their answers in the chart.

Students discuss the four questions with their partner, making a note of the key ideas.

Speak and share

Put students in small groups and ask them to review the *Grammar* and *Speaking* skills pages. Set a time limit for the discussion, and highlight that you will be listening for conditional sentences, and explanations of unknown words. As students discuss their ideas, monitor and note successful and less successful language use in the two key areas.

Go through the answers with the class. Encourage students to share ideas, and ask each other further questions.

Have a feedback session on language use. Share the examples you noted, and highlight effective language use. For less successful language use, encourage peer correction.

Reflect

Students reflect on the question alone. Ask them to make a note of their reflections, and to share useful strategies they identify with the class.

REVIEW

Wordlist

Students work in pairs or small groups to work through the *Wordlist*, checking that they all remember what each word or phrase means, how to pronounce it, and how it was used in the unit. Go through the list carefully with the class.

Academic words review

Students work through the sentences, check in pairs, and then feed back to the class.

ANSWERS
1 factor   2 revise   3 complement   4 specific
5 tense

Unit review

Students work through the list alone to decide what they can and can't do. They discuss their answers in pairs, including what they remember from the unit about each point. Finally, open up the discussion to include the whole class. Pay particular attention to any boxes that the students didn't check. Explore with them ways of overcoming any remaining problems.

Extra research task

As a take-home activity, ask students to research or find a person who has been, or is successful in a high-pressure job. They should identify the strategies used by the person, and the factors that helped the person to succeed when under pressure. The research can be presented in a series of mini-talks at the start of the next lesson.

7 FEAR

LISTENING 1	Recognizing organizational phrases
LISTENING 2	Listening for problems and solutions
STUDY SKILL	Increasing confidence when speaking
VOCABULARY	Suffixes -ful and -less
GRAMMAR	The present perfect tense with adverbs
SPEAKING	Managing questions

Warm-up

With books closed, write *fear* on the board. Then tell a personal story about a time when you were afraid. (Choose a story which isn't too serious, and that has a happy ending if possible.) Describe the symptoms you felt, using the four areas of the body from the infographic (*heart, muscles, time, hair*). When you finish, ask students to retell the story to you. Elicit the symptoms of fear that you described and write the key words on the board. Students then describe a time they were afraid to their partner. They should include why they felt afraid and how they felt, using the key words on the board as appropriate. Monitor and encourage follow-up questions. For feedback, ask *Would you be afraid in the situation your partner described? Why / why not?*

Discussion point >

Students read through the infographic, and check the meaning of vocabulary as required. They then discuss the three questions with a partner. Have the class give feedback. Encourage discussion of question 2 with follow-up questions (e.g., *Why are we afraid of these things? Are these fears the same for all ages?*). Ask two or three volunteers to share stories of when they are afraid. Encourage discussion of these situations (e.g., *Would you be afraid in this situation? Have you experienced something similar?*).

VIDEO >

Before you watch

Students work in pairs to match the words to the definitions.

> ANSWERS
> **1** c **2** a **3** b **4** d **5** e

While you watch

Focus students on the photo of the slide. Then allow students time to read through the statements. Check vocabulary as necessary. Play the video. Students compare answers with a partner, and then play the video again as required. For those sentences which are false, ask students to correct the statement to make it true.

> ANSWERS
> **1** F (The slide is on the outside of a tall building.)
> **2** T **3** T
> **4** F (Only one person says she has a fear of heights.)
> **5** F (It is not well-known for its tall buildings.)

See page 109 for the video script.

After you watch

Ask students to explain the difference between *fear* and *phobia* (**Possible answer:** *a phobia is a very strong fear that can control people's lives*). Students discuss the questions with a partner. In whole-class feedback, list the phobias on the board and keep a tally of student answers to find out the most common phobia.

LISTENING 1 >

Fear of public speaking

A Vocabulary preview

1   Students work alone to match the words in bold with the correct definitions. Allow time for students to compare in pairs, and then check as a class.

> ANSWERS
> **1** g **2** h **3** b **4** e **5** f **6** d **7** c **8** a

2   Students answer the questions in pairs. Ask students to report back on their partner's answers in whole-class feedback.

Extension activity

Students write questions using the words in bold from Exercise 1 which are not used in the questions in Exercise 2 (*connect, limit, memorize, athletes, topic*) (e.g., *How do you connect with people when you give a presentation?*). The students then mingle and ask other students their questions. They then report back the most interesting answer to each question to the class.

B Before you listen
Activating prior knowledge

Students discuss the questions in pairs. Monitor and listen to the fears the students have. Encourage discussion between the pairs, and listen sensitively. Avoid whole-class feedback with your class, unless you feel it is appropriate, as some students may not wish to share their fears on this topic with the class.

C Global listening
Recognizing organizational phrases

With books closed, write on the board *Today, I'm going to talk about …* Tell the students they are going to listen to a talk about public speaking. Ask the students to first identify the different stages of a talk (**Answer:** *introduction, main body, and conclusion*). Then ask students for suggestions of phrases that speakers use to organize their ideas in a talk. Write the phrases on the board, reformulating as necessary. Then allow students time to read through the *Recognizing organizational phrases* box, comparing the phrases with those on the board.

Students read through the sentences, underline the organizational phrases, and predict the order of the sentences. Play the audio, and then allow time for students to compare answers in pairs, and then check answers as class.

AUDIO SCRIPT

 Track 7.1

SPEAKER: Hello everyone. Today I'm going to talk about the fear of public speaking. First, I'll discuss three interesting facts about public speaking. Then I'll provide five tips for facing this fear. At the end of my talk, I'll tell you where you can get more information on this topic. Let's get started. If you have any questions, feel free to ask.

So, here are three facts about the fear of public speaking. The first one is that, according to some surveys, it is the biggest fear people have. It's even more common than the fear of dying. In fact, about 75% of people say they have this fear.

STUDENT 1: Have you ever had this fear?

SPEAKER: Well, yes, I have. I gave a talk last year before a large group and I felt very nervous, but I'm not nervous today, you know. The second fact is that men and women are affected equally. That may not be surprising, but what may be surprising is that men are more likely than women to find ways to deal with their fear. And third, having this fear can have a negative effect on your career if you don't do anything about it. It can even affect other aspects of your life. But there is good news. You can do something

about it. Let's now look at some tips for facing this fear. There are several things you can do.

One—start small. Find a few friends to practice with and then practice again with a larger group. If you start small, you will begin to feel more confident.

STUDENT 2: So, like, how small should the group be?

SPEAKER: Experts say the size of the audience makes no difference. When you actually do speak in public, just imagine the group is small.

Two—be prepared. Knowing your material will reduce your fear. If you don't know your material, you will be anxious and possibly get lost. Practice your presentation and time yourself. Also, have more material in case you finish early—I mean, not a lot, just a little extra.

Three—don't memorize everything. No one wants to hear a memorized speech.

STUDENT 3: Sorry, but what is wrong with memorizing?

SPEAKER: I think it's kind of boring for the audience. It also shows you aren't confident. Remembering the main points and examples is enough.

Four—reduce stress. You see, for many, the minute just before you speak is the most fearful. Find what works for you. Close your eyes. Laugh. Try what some athletes do. They imagine a positive result and breathe deeply to reduce their stress.

Five—involve the audience.

STUDENT 4: And, uh, how do you do that?

SPEAKER: Well, for example, before you begin your presentation, talk to a few people in the audience. This shows you are friendly and relaxed. You might want to take questions from the audience during your presentation too, like I'm doing now.

Let me conclude by providing you with some additional information. There are a lot of resources out there for this kind of thing; you can find books on facing your fears in the local library or at any bookstore. I would recommend a book called *Be Prepared, Be Confident* by Dr. Ricardo Lopez.

STUDENT 5: Do you know when that book was published?

SPEAKER: I'm sorry, but I don't have the answer to that. I'll try and find out. Now, does anyone else have any questions. Yes?

STUDENT 6: Yes. Why shouldn't someone memorize a presentation?

SPEAKER: I think I've already answered that. No one wants to hear a memorized speech, because it's frankly, boring. It's OK to memorize the key points but …

ANSWERS
1 c 2 e 3 b 4 g 5 d 6 a 7 f

D Close listening

Listening for details

1   Give students time to review the notes and the words in the box. Check the meanings of the words in the box, and elicit which were in the *Vocabulary preview* (**Answer:** *audience, memorize*). Students could work together to predict where the words go. Then play the audio. Allow time for students to compare their answers and complete their notes, before going through the answers as a class.

AUDIO SCRIPT

 Track 7.1

ANSWERS
1 Facts   2 fear   3 equally   4 Men   5 negative
6 Tips   7 time   8 memorize   9 main   10 stress
11 audience   12 Prepared

2   Ask students how the speaker connected with the students (**Answer**: *by answering questions throughout the talk*). Allow students time to read through the different ways of handling questions. Then play the excerpts. Students compare their answers in pairs. Play the audio again as required. Go through the answers with the class.

AUDIO SCRIPT

 Track 7.2

1

SPEAKER: It's even more common than the fear of dying. In fact, about 75% of people say they have this fear.

STUDENT 1:   Have you ever had this fear?

SPEAKER: Well, yes. I have. I gave a talk last year before a large group and I felt very nervous, but I'm not nervous today, you know …

2

SPEAKER: Find a few friends to practice with and then practice again with a larger group. If you start small, you will begin to feel more confident.

STUDENT 2:   So, like, how small should the group be?

SPEAKER: Experts say the size of the audience makes no difference. When you actually do speak in public, just imagine the group is small.

3

SPEAKER: Don't memorize everything. No one wants to hear a memorized speech.

STUDENT 3:   Sorry, but what is wrong with memorizing?

SPEAKER: I think it's kind of boring for the audience. It also shows you aren't confident. Remembering the main points and examples is enough.

4

SPEAKER: Involve the audience.

STUDENT 4:   And, uh, how do you do that?

SPEAKER: Well, for example, before you begin your presentation, talk to a few people in the audience. This shows you are friendly and relaxed. You might want to take questions from the audience during your presentation too, like I'm doing now.

5

STUDENT 5:   Do you know when that book was published?

SPEAKER: I'm sorry, but I don't have the answer to that. I'll try and find out.

6

SPEAKER: Now, does anyone else have any questions? Yes?

STUDENT 6:   Yes. Why shouldn't someone memorize a presentation?

PRESENTER: I think I've already answered that. No one wants to hear a memorized speech, because it's frankly, boring.

ANSWERS
1 c   2 e   3 b   4 a   5 f   6 d

E Critical thinking

Critical thinking involves evaluating ideas and justifying conclusions. In this exercise, students evaluate the tips for helping people with a fear of public speaking. Monitor and encourage students to justify their answers, with the other members in the group using the *Why / why not?* prompt.

Pronunciation for listening
Listening for conversation fillers

With books closed, introduce this section by saying *Um, so we're going to look at conversation fillers or something.* Then ask students what you said, and write the sentence on the board. Write the fillers in a different color, or underline them. Analyze the sentence and the fillers, and ask for suggestions as to why we use fillers. Then give students time to read through the *Listening for conversation fillers* box, comparing their ideas with those in the book.

1 Students work in pairs to identify the fillers. Students then practice saying the sentences with their partner.

> **ANSWERS**
>
> **1** you know **2** So, like, **3** I mean, **4** kind of
> **5** You see, **6** And, um,

2 Go through the task with students, highlighting that the fillers are not included in the written conversations. Students then listen and check the sentences with fillers. They could also make a note of the fillers used.

> **AUDIO SCRIPT**
> _____
>
> 🎧 **Track 7.3**
>
> 1 **A:** So, like how did you find the lecture?
>   **B:** It was pretty interesting.
> 2 **A:** How can I get over my fear of public speaking?
>   **B:** Why don't you practice your presentation in front a mirror, or something?
> 3 **A:** I've always been terrified of snakes.
>   **B:** And, um, what do you think causes that?
> 4 **A:** What are your fears? I mean, what are you afraid of?
>   **B:** I'm not afraid of much, but I don't like driving fast.
> 5 **A:** How do you deal with your fear of flying?
>   **B:** I listen to music and … and just kind of try not to think about it.
> 6 **A:** I'm terrified of crowded places. What can I do?
>   **B:** Well, it's not, you know, something you can get over right away.

> **ANSWERS**
> _____
>
> **1** A **2** B **3** B **4** A **5** B **6** B

3 Students listen and write the sentences without writing the fillers. Ask students to check in pairs, and then listen again. Go through the answers with the class.

> **AUDIO SCRIPT**
> _____
>
> 🎧 **Track 7.4**
>
> 1 It's OK, you know, to have fears.
> 2 I mean, everyone is afraid of something.
> 3 Talk about your fears with a friend, or something.
> 4 So, like, don't let your fears affect your career.

> **ANSWERS**
> _____
>
> **1** It's OK to have fears.
> **2** Everyone is afraid of something.
> **3** Talk about your fears with a friend.
> **4** Don't let your fears affect your career.

LISTENING 2 >

Phobias
A Vocabulary preview

1 Students work alone to match the words to the definitions in bold. Students compare their answers in pairs, and then check as a class.

> **ANSWERS**
> _____
>
> **1** b **2** h **3** f **4** a **5** c **6** d **7** g **8** e

2 Students work in pairs to complete each sentence with a word from Exercise 1. Go through the answers with the class.

> **ANSWERS**
> _____
>
> **1** frightened **2** powerless **3** certain **4** awful
> **5** control **6** seek **7** overcome **8** impair

> **Extension activity**
>
> Write the eight words from Exercise 1 on the board. Students work in pairs. Student A sits with their back to the board. Student B describes and defines each word (choosing in a random order from the board) without saying the actual word. Student A should guess the word by writing it down, with Student B indicating when the word is correct. After the set time, award one point for each correct answer. Students then swap roles.

B Before you listen

Activating prior knowledge

Students review the pictures. Ask them to rank the images in order of how much they fear them. Students then work with a partner to discuss the pictures, and explain their rankings. In whole-class feedback, keep a tally of student answers to see which of the four things is most feared.

C Global listening

Listening for key words

Review the word box with the students, checking the meanings as necessary. Play the audio while students circle the phobias mentioned. Go through the answers with the class.

AUDIO SCRIPT

 Track 7.5

HOST: Hello and welcome to this week's episode of *To Your Health*. I've invited Dr. Kristin Patterson, an expert on phobias, to speak with us today. Good morning and welcome.

DR. PATTERSON: It's great to be here.

HOST: Let's start out with a definition. What is a phobia? Is it just a fear of something?

DR. PATTERSON: A phobia is more than just a fear. Everyone has certain fears. This is normal and a good thing because a reasonable fear of something dangerous helps keep us safe. There's a reason to be afraid of some snakes, for example. But this is not a phobia of snakes. A phobia is *not* reasonable. You fear a snake because it may be harmful. A phobia of snakes, on the other hand, may mean that you can't hike in the forest because you fear you will see a snake. You become frightened of seeing a snake on TV or at the zoo. It's difficult to even look at a photo of one. You feel without power because a phobia has a serious impact on your life. It can stop you from doing what you normally would do.

HOST: Are phobias common?

DR. PATTERSON: Yes. During their lifetime, more than 10% of people will develop a phobia. One of the most common phobias is the fear of public speaking. Speaking in front of others causes a lot of stress for many of us. But there are many other kinds of phobias, such as the fear of water and fear of spiders.

HOST: Oh, I've always hated spiders!

DR. PATTERSON: You have? Does this impair your day-to-day activities?

HOST: Uh, well, I once saw a spider in my closet and didn't open it for two weeks.

DR. PATTERSON: You know you may have a phobia of spiders. We can work on how to overcome that a bit later. So, how do people react when they're confronted with a phobia? Often a person's heart will beat faster. It may be difficult for them to breathe. They might get a sick feeling. Other people with phobias may feel helpless and start to panic.

HOST: I see.

DR. PATTERSON: I had a patient recently that had a terrible phobia of elevators. Let's call her Maggie. One problem Maggie faced was that a recent job promotion required her to move her office from the first floor in her building up to the tenth floor. She was certain that the elevator would break while she was inside, or she'd not have enough air to breathe, or the elevator would fall. Her friends tried to tell her everything would be fine, but it was pointless. She had a strong fear of elevators.

ANSWERS

elevators   public speaking   snakes   spiders   water

D Close listening

Listening for problems and solutions

Allow students time to read through the *Listening for problems and solutions* box and study the information. Then with books closed, elicit the phrases for stating problems and offering solutions. Ask students how they should be listening, and what they should be thinking when listening to solutions (**Answer:** *critically / how well-supported are the solutions in terms of arguments and reasons*).

1   Allow students time to read through the questions, and make a note of any predicted answers. Students then listen to the first half of *Phobias* again, and answer the questions. Go through the answers with the class.

AUDIO SCRIPT

 Track 7.5

ANSWERS
1 phobias   **2** It helps keep us safe.   **3** heart beats faster, hard to breathe, might get a sick feeling
4 elevators   **5** Her new office was on the tenth floor.

---

2   Allow students time to read through the solutions and recall, or predict which are mentioned. Then play the second half of *Phobias*. Students check the solutions mentioned. They compare their answers with a partner. Go through the answers with the class.

AUDIO SCRIPT

 Track 7.6

HOST: That's awful! So, have you been able to help Maggie with her problem? Were you able to find a solution?

DR. PATTERSON: We were successful but it took a long time. The first step was that Maggie needed to realize she needed help. Surprisingly, people sometimes don't want to seek help, or they don't know where to get help. Phobias may be painful but we can almost always help people with phobias. It's much easier than people think. Maggie and I did some techniques together to help her relax. These techniques were useful because they helped her avoid the physical symptoms. I taught her to take slow, deep breaths. Then she was able to think more clearly about the situation. We then discussed each thought that scared her. It was interesting that she never actually experienced a problem with an elevator. And we talked about how it's always possible to breathe in an elevator. I was worried that she might also have a fear of small places, but this wasn't the case.

HOST: So, how did Maggie get to the point where she could take the elevator to work?

DR. PATTERSON: First, she had to face her fears. After talking about her fears, and after learning to relax, she started to watch the elevator. In the beginning, she just watched people getting on, getting off, smiling, and talking with others. The next day, she watched it again. But then we stepped in the elevator, together. It didn't go anywhere—we just let the doors open and close automatically. She was nervous, but by breathing deeply and relaxing, she was in control. The next day, we repeated the first two steps, and then finally took the elevator up, but only one floor. We repeated this over several days, adding one floor each day.

HOST: So, did she get to her new office?

DR. PATTERSON: She did. I went to her office on the tenth floor and called her. I asked her to go into the elevator. She went in, she pressed the tenth floor button, and two minutes later—do you know what happened? She stepped out of the elevator. By doing all of those things, she's been able to overcome her phobia. It took just a few days. Now, about that spider in your closet …

HOST: Um, oh, I'm afraid we're about out of time. Join us on our next podcast when we talk about…

ANSWERS
✓ realizing she needed help
✓ techniques to help her relax
✓ deep breathing
✓ talking about what scared her
✓ watching the elevator
✓ standing in the elevator
✓ taking the elevator up only one floor
✓ taking the elevator up one floor at a time
✓ taking the elevator to the tenth floor

E Critical thinking

As outlined in the Close listening skills box, students should consider solutions critically in order to evaluate their benefit. They need to consider the reasons for adopting a particular solution, and other possible considerations such as practicality, cost, immediacy of effect, etc.

In question 1, students evaluate the solutions offered by Dr. Patterson. They can also consider other possible solutions for the elevator phobia and for phobias in general.

Students evaluate the extent of fears they experience. Before discussing the actual fears, students should work in groups to identify the criteria for something being termed a phobia (**Possible answers:** *changes your life / controls behavior / very strong fear / no rational reason for fear*). Students share their criteria with the class, and then return to working in their groups to evaluate their own fears.

STUDY SKILLS

Increasing confidence when speaking

Warm-up

Explain to students that when you have to speak in public, you feel afraid (or, if you don't, say someone you know does). Ask for their advice, and make a note of their tips on the board. Ask them why they think each tip will work, and ask them if they have any experience with using the tip.

Students read through the *Increasing confidence when speaking* box. If the *Warm-up* was used, they can identify which tips in the box they already mentioned.

Extension activity

Students share their own opinions and experiences with the tips. Ask them to identify which they have used, and also the top three most valuable tips. They then work in pairs to share their personal experiences, and try to agree on the top three tips overall.

1 Students work together to review the quotes, and match them to the tips in the *Study skills* box. Go through the answers with the class.

ANSWERS
a 5 **b** 2 **c** 1 **d** 4 **e** 6 **f** 3

2 Students discuss the questions in pairs. After discussing both questions, put pairs together. Students report what their partner told them for question 1, checking they got the details correct. The group then identifies a list of qualities and strategies which can make a person confident when speaking.

VOCABULARY >

Vocabulary development
Suffixes -*ful* and -*less*

With books closed, draw the diagram on the board and label it. Say the word *beauty* and point at -*ful,* and -*less* to elicit suggestions as to where to write the word. Write *beautiful* in the correct place. Then do the same with *job*, and finally with *fear*. Add the other words to the side of the board and ask students to come to the board to add the words to the correct place in the diagram. Avoid providing any assistance at this point, and allow incorrect answers. Then students open their books, and read through the information in the *Suffixes* -ful *and* -less box. They compare the diagram in the book to the one on the board, and come to the board to make any necessary corrections.

1 Students work alone to complete the diagram. They then compare their answers with a partner's. Again, invite students to come to the board to add the words from this exercise to the diagram which is already there.

> ANSWERS
> careful / careless   harmful / harmless   helpful / helpless
> pointless   powerful / powerless   truthful   wonderful
> worthless

2 Students work alone to complete the sentences with the words in the box and the correct suffixes. Allow time for students to compare their answers in pairs, and then check as a class.

> ANSWERS
> **1** wonderful   **2** fearful   **3** harmful   **4** stressful
> **5** successful   **6** pointless   **7** homeless

VOCABULARY >

Academic words

1 Students work alone to match the words to the definitions. Ask students to check in pairs, and to identify the stress pattern for each word.

> ANSWERS
> **1** c   **2** f   **3** a   **4** e   **5** h   **6** b   **7** g   **8** d

2 Students complete the questions with the words from Exercise 1. Go through the answers with the class.

> ANSWERS
> **1** technique   **2** author   **3** impact   **4** definition
> **5** affect   **6** survey   **7** resource   **8** automatic

3 Students choose four questions to ask their partner. Encourage them to ask follow-up questions to extend the discussion. Ask students to report the most surprising information they found out.

SPEAKING >

Speaking model

Read through the aims of the *Speaking* section with the students. Remind the students that all parts of this section build towards the successful completion of the final task. Ask them to identify an example of the *present perfect* in the aims (**Answer:** *you've had to solve*).

A Analyze

1 Ask students to look quickly through the model, and identify the context (**Possible answer:** *a single speaker is giving a talk about a personal experience*). Students then read the model in detail, and add the five sentences to the correct places. Go through the answers with the class.

> ANSWERS
> **1** b   **2** e   **3** d   **4** c   **5** a

2 Students analyze the organization of the presentation in pairs. Go through the answers with the class.

> ANSWERS
> **1** He summarizes what he is going to say.
> **2** He presents his problem.
> **3** He explains his problem in more detail.
> **4** He asks if the audience has any questions.

3 Students work individually to underline the examples of the present perfect. Ask students to check in pairs, and then check as a class.

> ANSWERS
>
> I have found,   I have made,   I have already made,
> I haven't met,   I still haven't had
> Something that happened in the past.

B Discuss

Students work in pairs to summarize how the speaker handled the problem. Monitor and check understanding as students do this. Students then describe a problem they have dealt with. Put pairs together, and ask the students to summarize their partner's problem for the new pair.

GRAMMAR >>

The present perfect tense with adverbs

With books closed, write the following on the board: *Have you ever spoken in public? I've spoken in public three times.* Ask students *Do we know when I spoke?* (**Answer:** *no*), then ask *Will I speak in public in the future?* (**Answer:** *don't know*). Ask *What verb tense is this?* (**Answer:** *present perfect*). Then say *I've never spoken in public*, and ask *What type of word is never?* (**Answer:** *adverb*), and *How many times have I spoken in public?* (**Answer:** *0*). Then students open their books, and read through *The present perfect tense with adverbs* box. Elicit that the position of the adverb changes, depending on the actual adverb used.

1 Ask students to study and then cover the skills box. Students then work alone to rewrite the sentences with the adverb. Students check their answers with a partner's, and then use the box to confirm.

> ANSWERS
>
> 1 Sally has already given that speech three times.
> 2 Have you ever seen a 10-centimeter-long spider?
> 3 Jeff hasn't practiced his talk yet.
> 4 I still haven't spoken with a doctor about my fear of heights.
> 5 Have they taken their final exams yet?
> 6 They have never felt comfortable in small, closed spaces.

2 With the sentence already on the board, elicit the grammatical structure of the *present perfect* (**Answer:** *have* + past participle). Students then work alone to write the sentences using the prompts in parentheses. Go through the answers with the class.

> ANSWERS
>
> 1 Samantha has already uploaded a video of her talk.
> 2 Glenn has not told anyone about his fear of flying yet.
> 3 Iris still has not shared her fears with her friends.
> 4 I have never met anyone with a fear of cats.

Extension activity

Students take part in a *Find someone who …* mingling exercise. Each student writes five questions using the present perfect and "*ever*" (e.g., *Have you ever performed in front of an audience?*). They then mingle with other students, asking and answering questions. They should make a note of each answer, and any extra information. Before they mingle, model an answer for the class. Invite a student to ask you a question, and reply using adverbs as appropriate (e.g., *No, I haven't done that yet, but I plan to …*).

SPEAKING >>

Speaking skill
Managing questions

Ask students to read through the *Managing questions* box. Model the language in the skills box. Give students time to practice the phrases in pairs. Monitor the activity and assist as required.

1 Read through the task with students, and then play the audio. Give students time to compare their answers in pairs before playing the audio again.

AUDIO SCRIPT

🎧 **Track 7.7**

1

PRESENTER: Let's get started. If you have any questions, feel free to ask.

2

STUDENT 5:   Do you know when that book was published?

PRESENTER: I'm sorry, but I don't have the answer to that. I'll try and find out.

3

STUDENT 6:   Yes. Why shouldn't someone memorize a presentation?

PRESENTER: I think I've already answered that.

2 Each group selects one topic, and then works together to brainstorm ideas. They then divide the ideas between the group members. Each group member then prepares to speak for one minute. Group members present their part of the talk to the rest of the group, using a phrase to say they will take questions at the end. They then use further phrases to deal with the questions. Monitor the activity and assist as required, praising use of the target language.

Exam skill

The IELTS Speaking Test includes giving a two-minute talk on a given topic. The candidate has one minute to prepare for this. It is good practice for students to get used to preparing quickly for short informal talks, making sure they make full use of the available time to prepare. They can make notes, identify key vocabulary, and organize their ideas in this time.

PRONUNCIATION

Pronunciation for speaking
Pausing and pacing

With books closed, model the two examples from the *Pausing and pacing* box, the first with the correct pauses, and the second with the incorrect pauses. Elicit differences and the effect these have on the listener. While students are sharing their ideas, write the key words *pausing* and *pacing* on the board, along with other useful terms (**Example:** *breath, natural, chunk, unnatural, speed*).

Students open their books and read through the information in the skills box.

1 Students listen and follow the text in the book, listening for pauses.

AUDIO SCRIPT

 Track 7.8

First, she had to face her fears. After talking about her fears, and after learning to relax, she started to watch the elevator. In the beginning, she just watched people getting on, getting off, smiling, and talking with others. The next day, she watched it again. But then we stepped into the elevator, together. It didn't go anywhere—we just let the doors open and close automatically. She was nervous, but by breathing deeply and relaxing, she was in control. The next day, we repeated the first two steps, and then finally took the elevator up, but only one floor. We repeated this over several days, adding one floor each day.

2 Students listen again and add the arrows to show faster and slower speech.

AUDIO SCRIPT

 Track 7.8

3 Students practice reading the text in pairs, following the pause marks and arrows. Monitor the activity, helping students to remember to pace and pause where necessary.

Extension activity

Students record themselves saying the text, following the pausing and speed marks. They then work with a partner to evaluate their recordings. They can first establish a checklist for evaluation (e.g., *appropriate speed / appropriate pauses / natural / clear / confident*).

Speaking task

Warm-up

Test students on the content of this unit. Put students into teams, and give them a set amount of time to review the unit (e.g., 20 minutes). Tell them what the test will focus on (e.g., *information in the listenings / grammar / vocabulary / phrases / a combination*). As students review the unit, prepare questions. Students then answer the questions in a quiz format. Award one point for each correct answer.

Read the task with the students. Then give the class time to review the unit. They should make a note of useful vocabulary, phrases, and grammar which will help with the final task.

Brainstorm and plan

Students discuss their experiences with the problems in the box, and how they tried to solve them. Students then work alone to select one of the problems they discussed and make notes on it, following the diagram in the book. Monitor the activity, and assist as necessary to ensure students make a full set of notes. Students then continue to work alone to use their notes to prepare a presentation.

Extension activity

If recording facilities are available, students record their practice interviews, and watch them to check their pausing and speed of delivery.

Speak and share

Students work in groups and take turns giving their presentations. When watching the presentations, students think of and ask questions during, or after the presentation, as requested by the presenter.

As students give their presentations, monitor and note successful and less successful language use in the key areas.

Students then share with their group members what they like about each presentation.

Have a feedback session on language use. Share the examples you noted, and highlight effective language use. For less successful language use, encourage peer correction, and help the students to reformulate the language.

Reflect

Give students time to reflect on their own presentations, making a note of their answers. Then ask students to share their reflections with a partner. Monitor the activity, and join the discussions as appropriate.

Wordlist

Students work in pairs or small groups to work through the *Wordlist*, checking that they all remember what each word or phrase means, how to pronounce it, and how it was used in the unit. Go through the list carefully with the class.

Academic words review

Students work through the sentences, check their answers in pairs, and then check as a class.

> ANSWERS
> **1** definition **2** survey **3** technique **4** resource
> **5** impact

Unit review

Students work through the list alone to decide what they can and can't do. They discuss their answers in pairs, including what they remember from the unit about each point. Finally, open up the discussion to include the whole class. Pay particular attention to any boxes that the students didn't check. Explore with them ways of overcoming any remaining problems.

Extra research task

As a take-home activity, ask students to create a survey about phobias, using the *present perfect* in at least two questions (e.g., *Have you ever not done something because of fear?*). They conduct the survey with four people, and then report on the findings in the following lesson.

8 STORIES

LISTENING 1	Listening for the order of events
LISTENING 2	Adding details to a diagram
STUDY SKILL	Finding your creative streak
VOCABULARY	Using descriptive adjectives
GRAMMAR	The past progressive
SPEAKING	Using sentence adverbs

Warm-up

Tell a short, simple, well-known fairy tale, appropriate for the class you are working with, such as *Cinderella*. Then ask students if they know the story. They may have read the story, or seen a film of it when they were young. Then ask students to think of another story other people in the class may have heard of. Invite students to tell the story (briefly), and see how many students recognize it, or have a similar story in their culture.

Discussion point

With books closed, write the following words on the board: *senses, multiple parts of the brain, chemical, system, emotional event, process, pattern, science.* Check the meaning of the words, and ask students how they think these words relate to the topic of the unit *Stories.* Listen and encourage students to expand on their ideas. Then give students time to read through the infographic in their books. Ask students to explain the information using the key words on the board.

Students discuss the questions in pairs. Monitor and encourage the sharing of stories. At this point, make a mental note of the use of the past tenses to tell stories. The grammar focus of the unit is the *past progressive,* so listen for any uses of the tense at this point. However, if you choose to make an actual note of language use at this point in order to have whole-class feedback, focus on the *simple past* to consolidate the use of this tense before students focus on the past progressive.

Invite one or two students to retell a story from their childhood, or a story they have read, heard, or seen recently. Then have a show of hands to see the preferred interaction of the class with stories: reading, writing, listening to, or telling.

VIDEO

Before you watch

Focus students' attention on the picture and ask questions (e.g., *Where is the man? Why? Why do you think this man is called the French Spiderman?*).

Check the meaning of the words with the students, or allow time for them to do so with their dictionaries. Students discuss what they might see in the video.

While you watch

Allow time for students to read the sentences to be completed. Play the video. Students complete the sentences and then check as a whole class. Play the video again as appropriate.

> ANSWERS
> **1** wheel **2** safety gear **3** the weather **4** slippery

See page 109 for the video script.

After you watch

1 Students work alone to make notes on the story, using the five questions to guide their note-taking. Monitor and encourage students to be detailed with their notes. Play the video with the sound off as they do this.

2 Students retell the story with a partner. They can share the story by talking about alternating questions. Alternatively, you could call time after one minute, and then the second student takes over the story telling. Keep doing this until the story is finished.

LISTENING 1

A travel story

A Vocabulary preview

1 Students work alone to match the words to the definitions. Allow time for students to compare answers in pairs. Then go through the answers with the class.

> ANSWERS
> **1** g **2** e **3** c **4** b **5** a **6** f **7** h **8** d

2 Students work alone to complete the sentences with the words from Exercise 1. Go through the answers with the class.

3   Students review the sentences with a partner and
     discuss which they agree with. Monitor and encourage
     students to ask follow-up questions to find out more
     about their partner's opinion. Ask students to report
     back on the sentences they most disagreed on.

B Before you listen
Activating prior knowledge

Warm-up

Ask students to close their eyes and think about their last
vacation. Ask questions to help them to visualize it (e.g.,
*Where were you? Why did you go? Who were you with? What
did you see? What was the weather like? What did you eat /
feel / smell / hear / do?*). Leave a pause between each
question. Then ask students to open their eyes and note
down everything they thought of. If they don't know the
word in English, they should note down the words in their
own language. Then when all the ideas are written, check
the words they don't know in a dictionary.

1   Students work in small groups to describe their last
     vacations. Monitor and encourage students to ask
     follow-up questions.

2   Students review the pictures, and then describe times
     they have been in these positions on a trip. If they have
     no personal experience with these things, they can talk
     about people they know.

C Global listening
Listening for main ideas

1   Tell students they are going to listen to someone
     describing a trip he went on to a friend. Allow time for
     students to read through the list. Then play the audio.
     Students compare answers in pairs before checking as
     a whole class.

AUDIO SCRIPT

 Track 8.1

MICHAEL: Hey Rachid. I wanted to ask you something.

RACHID: What's that?

MICHAEL: I remember you went to London last year. I was
curious how your trip went.

RACHID: Well, huh, that's a *funny* story. I almost didn't
make it to London at all.

MICHAEL: What do you mean?

RACHID: Well, a month before the trip, I bought my plane
ticket and reserved my accommodation. Then, I got my visa.
I changed money into the local currency on the day of my
flight. I had already confirmed my seat on the plane the night
before. I thought I had planned everything so well.

MICHAEL: Did something go wrong?

RACHID: Um, you could say that. My flight was at 11:30.
But that morning it was raining, so it was hard to get a cab.
I finally reserved one, and the taxi driver said he'd be there
soon. That's when things really started to go wrong. At 8:15
the driver called. He was running late. Then at 8:30 he called
again to say he was getting gas, and would be there soon.
After that he called again—at 8:45—to say he couldn't find my
place. I gave him directions.

MICHAEL: So what happened next?

RACHID: Clearly, I was starting to get *really* worried. Finally,
at ten o'clock my taxi arrived. I put my luggage in the car and
we left. I relaxed as we drove—I thought I still had enough
time. Then, I decided to check a few things. I had my wallet. I
had my tickets. But I couldn't find my passport.

MICHAEL: No way!

RACHID: Then I remembered. Before I booked the taxi, I was
organizing my bag. I took the passport out and put it on the
bed. I never put it back.

MICHAEL: How awful! So, what did you do?

RACHID: Obviously, I asked the driver to go back to my
house. I ran inside, got the passport, and then we went to
the airport. The airport was busy that day, and the lines were
long. I finally got to the airline check-in counter. It was closed.
I was too late. I missed my flight.

MICHAEL: Oh no!

RACHID: Yeah, I didn't know what to do. I felt so down! I
couldn't afford to buy a new ticket.

MICHAEL: So, …

RACHID: Well, I went to the help desk. A very friendly woman
there helped me. She checked my ticket and looked to see
if there were other flights. There was only one other flight to
London. It left three hours later.

MICHAEL: And there were seats?

RACHID: Luckily, there was one seat.

MICHAEL: So, you got it?

RACHID: Yes. I only had to pay a small fee to change the time
on my ticket. I was so happy. I got the ticket, went through
immigration to get my passport stamped, and after a few
hours got on the flight.

MICHAEL: That's great.

RACHID: But that's not the end of the story. It was a tiny
middle seat. But that was fine. Then I realized there was no
entertainment system—no movies, or TV to pass the time.
Then, while I was getting comfortable, a man came up to me.
He introduced himself and said his wife was sitting next to
me. He asked me to change seats with him, and I said, "Sure!"

MICHAEL: Really?

RACHID: And get this! He had a seat in first class, but he couldn't get a seat for his wife there. He offered me his first-class seat.

MICHAEL: Did you take it?

RACHID: Of course! I would have changed seats with him anyway, but first class? It was wonderful. The seat was enormous!

MICHAEL: And you made it to London in time for the conference?

RACHID: Thankfully, I did.

ANSWERS
- ✓ how he got to the airport
- ✓ why he was late for the airport
- ✓ something he forgot to pack
- ✓ where he sat on the plane

---

2 Students review the summaries with a partner and select the best one.

ANSWER
b

D Close listening

Listening for the order of events

Read through the *Listening for the order of events* box with the students, and ask questions to check understanding.

1 Allow students time to review the *Listening for the order of events* box, and the exercise text. Then play the first part of the story. Students number the events in order, and then compare with a partner's answers.

AUDIO SCRIPT

🎧 **Track 8.2**

MICHAEL: Hey Rachid. I wanted to ask you something.

RACHID: What's that?

MICHAEL: I remember you went to London last year. I was curious how your trip went.

RACHID: Well, huh, that's a *funny* story. I almost didn't make it to London at all.

MICHAEL: What do you mean?

RACHID: Well, a month before the trip, I bought my plane ticket, and reserved my accommodation. Then, I got my visa. I changed money into the local currency on the day of my flight. I had already confirmed my seat on the plane the night before. I thought I had planned everything so well.

MICHAEL: Did something go wrong?

RACHID: Um, you could say that. My flight was at 11:30. But that morning it was raining, so it was hard to get a cab. I finally reserved one, and the taxi driver said he'd be there soon. That's when things really started to go wrong. At 8:15 the driver called. He was running late. Then at 8:30 he called again to say he was getting gas, and would be there soon. After that he called again—at 8:45—to say he couldn't find my place. I gave him directions.

MICHAEL: So what happened next?

RACHID: Clearly, I was starting to get *really* worried. Finally, at ten o'clock my taxi arrived. I put my luggage in the car and we left. I relaxed as we drove—I thought I still had enough time. Then, I decided to check a few things. I had my wallet. I had my tickets. But I couldn't find my passport.

MICHAEL: No way!

RACHID: Then I remembered. Before I booked the taxi, I was organizing my bag. I took the passport out and put in on the bed. I never put it back.

MICHAEL: How awful! So, what did you do?

RACHID: Obviously, I asked the driver to go back to my house. I ran inside, got the passport, and then we went to the airport. The airport was busy that day, and the lines were long. I finally got to the airline check-in counter. It was closed. I was too late. I missed my flight.

ANSWERS
1 e He bought a plane ticket to London.
2 a He got a visa.
3 b He made sure his flight was confirmed.
4 f He changed money.
5 d He called to book a taxi.
6 c He went home to get his passport.

---

2 Allow students time to review the notes. Highlight that they are in the order the events happened in this story, and point out the direction of the arrows and the numbering. Play the audio. Students listen and complete the notes. Ask students to check in pairs, and then replay the audio if needed. Go through the answers with the class.

AUDIO SCRIPT

🎧 **Track 8.3**

MICHAEL: Oh no!

RACHID: Yeah, I didn't know what to do. I felt so down! I couldn't afford to buy a new ticket.

MICHAEL: So, …

RACHID: Well, I went to the help desk. A very friendly woman there helped me. She checked my ticket and looked to see if there were other flights. There was only one other flight to London. It left three hours later.

MICHAEL: And there were seats?

RACHID: Luckily, there was one seat.

MICHAEL: So, you got it?

RACHID: Yes. I only had to pay a small fee to change the time on my ticket. I was so happy. I got the ticket, went through immigration to get my passport stamped, and after a few hours got on the flight.

MICHAEL: That's great.

RACHID: But that's not the end of the story. It was a tiny middle seat. But that was fine. Then, I realized there was no entertainment system—no movies, or TV to pass the time. Then, while I was getting comfortable, a man came up to me. He introduced himself and said his wife was sitting next to me. He asked me to change seats with him, and I said, "Sure!"

MICHAEL: Really?

RACHID: And get this! He had a seat in first class, but he couldn't get a seat for his wife there. He offered me his first-class seat.

MICHAEL: Did you take it?

RACHID: Of course! I would have changed seats with him anyway, but first class? It was wonderful. The seat was enormous!

MICHAEL: And you made it to London in time for the conference?

RACHID: Thankfully, I did.

> ANSWERS
> **1** missed **2** woman **3** passport **4** waited
> **5** middle **6** change **7** first **8** conference

E Critical thinking

Evaluating in relation to criteria is a key part of critical thinking. Before making a judgement, criteria (i.e., what the judgement is based on) often needs to be established.

Ask students to discuss what makes a good storyteller.

Extension activity

Write on the board *A good storyteller is someone who …* and invite students to complete the sentence (e.g., *gives enough details, anticipates what the audience wants to know, doesn't talk for too long, gives the order of events clearly*). Establish a list of criteria on the board by writing several ways to complete the sentence, incorporating the students' ideas.

Students work in small groups to evaluate Rachid's storytelling. Share ideas as a whole class.

Finding your creative streak

Warm-up

With books closed, write on the board *Learning English is like riding a bike because you have to practice a lot*. Ask students to work in pairs to come up with other ways of completing the sentence after *because*. Then erase the entire sentence after *like*, and ask students to complete the sentence using the same structure. Highlight that students can think of fun ideas and be creative; there is no right or wrong answer. Students only need to find a way to justify their ideas. Share sentences as a whole class.

Allow time for students to read through the *Finding your creative streak* box. Explain that "Play" means to play with their ideas or subject by thinking of different ways, methods, and ideas behind it. Place students in small groups, and ask them to focus on one topic they have come across in their course work so far. Explain that they have to find out how each person in their group sees the topic they are focusing on by examining what it means for them outside an academic context. Have them think about: what the topic means for them, how they work with this topic, what they have learned about this topic. Discuss ideas as a class.

1 Students work with a partner to answer the questions creatively. Highlight that there is no one correct answer. Monitor and encourage student ideas. Then put pairs together, and ask the group to vote on their favorite sentence of the two for each question.

2 and 3 Students work alone to generate as many sentences as possible. They then compare answers with a partner, or in a small group, and check if they had any similar ideas. Ask them to choose their favorite sentences to share with the class.

Elements of a plot

A Vocabulary preview

1 Students work alone to match the words in bold in the sentences with the definitions. Ask students to compare in pairs, and then check as a class.

> ANSWERS
> **1** f **2** h **3** g **4** a **5** e **6** c **7** d **8** b

2 Students review the questions and identify the words used from Exercise 1 (**Answers:** *plot, conflict, literary, literature*). Students then discuss the questions with a partner.

B Before you listen

Activating prior knowledge

Students need to work with someone who knows the same story as they do. Ask students to name different stories (from books, movies, tradition, theater). Move students into different pairs or groups as necessary if common stories are not known. The pairs then use the guiding questions to make notes. Highlight that they will use these notes later in the unit, so they should ensure they have a complete set now, and store them safely.

C Global listening

Listening for key words

Extra support: Explain that Freytag was a 19th century German novelist who developed a diagram to analyze the common plots of stories in novels.

1   Highlight that the diagram shows the shape of a typical story, and that these stories can be divided into five parts. Students predict how to complete the diagram with the five elements.

> **ANSWERS**
> Exposition   Rising Action   Climax   Falling Action
> Resolution

AUDIO SCRIPT

 Track 8.4

PROFESSOR: Good afternoon, everyone, please take your seats. Welcome to the third day of our literature class. Today, we're talking about the plot. First, we'll define it. Then we'll examine this definition in more detail. Let's begin. Who can tell me what I mean by the plot?

STUDENT 1:   It's the events; what happens in a story.

PROFESSOR: OK. Yes, it's what happens. *Star Wars* filmmaker George Lucas once said, "Storytelling is about two things; it's about character and plot." It's that important. Without a plot, there's no story.

Now, you may be surprised that most stories—old ones, new ones, even those you may not be familiar with—have a lot in common with one another. There is something … ah, but before I get into that, does anyone know who Gustav Freytag was? No? Gustav Freytag was a German writer born in 1816. He looked at and studied many different plots that were found in literary works. He looked at the structures of ancient

Greek stories, as well as Shakespeare's plays. His analysis involved dividing a story into five parts, or five elements. And he developed something now called *Freytag's Pyramid*. I will draw it on the board. Let's look at each part in detail.

Every story must have a beginning. This is called *Exposition*.

STUDENT 2:   Again, please? It's called what?

PROFESSOR: *Exposition*. In the introduction, the speaker or writer needs to introduce the characters, and the relationships between them. In addition to characters, the speaker has to establish the setting—where the story takes place. This background information is important so that the listener becomes interested in the story and can follow it. Not too much usually happens in the beginning. There is the introduction of an initial conflict, or the main problem in the story. The real action begins in the next part.

The second part is known as the *Rising Action*. Here, the "plot thickens." Something happens that starts a series of events. Here, the main character faces a conflict. The character's conflict can be anything—nature, society, other people, or him, or herself. He or she tries to find a solution, so it is the part of the story that begins to get exciting as the tension builds and builds. Furthermore, it is usually the longest part of the story. A good story gets more and more exciting and interesting as the speaker builds to the next part.

The third part is the *Climax*, or the high point of the story. The *Climax* …

STUDENT 3:   Excuse me. Can you spell that?

PROFESSOR: Of course, C-L-I-M-A-X. The *Climax* is the main event our character faces. It's *definitely* the most exciting part of the story. It's the moment of greatest danger, greatest fear and/or emotion. There is so much drama. Will the hero fail? Will the hero be successful? It might be a *huge* fight. It might be a very exciting action scene, such as a car chase. It might be when the character learns something at last. For example, the hero's death in Shakespeare's *Hamlet*.

After the *Climax*, comes the next part—the *Falling Action*. Here, the character begins to deal with the conflict, perhaps to deal with any problem the conflict created. Imagine if after the *Climax* the story simply ended. How would we feel? We would not feel satisfied as we know there is more to the story. Now we see the effects of the actions that the character has taken.

Finally, we have the *Resolution*. We are very near the end of the story. There is less tension than before. There is no more conflict for our hero. All of our questions are answered. The story may conclude with a happy or sad ending. The characters have changed and may be back in their original situation. The main character may act differently, showing the results of the story's conflict.

So, to summarize, according to Freytag, a story should include all five of these elements in the correct order: *Exposition*, *Rising Action*, *Climax*, *Falling Action*, and *Resolution*. Now, let's look at and analyze one famous story, *The Boy Who Cried Wolf*. Work with the person next to you and …

2 Allow students time to review the descriptions of the five stages of a story. Play the audio. Then students complete the blanks, compare answers in pairs, and then check answers as a class.

ANSWERS
1 Exposition   2 Rising Action   3 Climax
4 Falling Action   5 Resolution

D Close listening

Listening to add details to a diagram

Allow time for students to read through the *Listening to add details to a diagram* box. Then ask *What are the benefits of diagrams?* Students should tell you in their own words (**Possible answers:** *to show you the main points of the talk, easy to copy, can add to them*).

1 Play the audio again. Students add notes to each stage of the diagram.

POSSIBLE ANSWERS
Exposition: introduces characters and their relationships, the setting, the background story
Rising Action: plot thickens, main character faces a conflict, tension builds
Climax: high point, main event, moment of greatest danger / fear / emotion
Falling Action: character begins to deal with conflict
Resolution: conflict ends, questions are answered

2 Students compare their answers in a group (their answers may vary), and then work together to complete the notes.

ANSWERS
1 five   2 relationships between them   3 conflict
4 exciting   5 effects   6 less   7 answered

3 Explain that students will hear a short story in five parts, and that they need to number the parts in order. Play the audio, and then allow students time to compare answers in pairs.

AUDIO SCRIPT

 Track 8.5

NARRATOR: Part a
There was once a young boy who lived near a dark forest. Every day he had to take care of his sheep. The young boy was lonely and bored.

NARRATOR: Part b
Soon after that, a wolf really *did* come into the village and began eyeing his sheep. He was extremely frightened. He cried, "Wolf! Help! This time, there really is a wolf!" The wolf came closer and closer to his sheep.

NARRATOR: Part c
When the boy complained, a wise old man in the village said, "Never lie. Even when a liar tells the truth, no one will believe him."

NARRATOR: Part d
He decided on a plan to relieve his boredom. He ran into the village shouting, "Wolf! Wolf!" People came to help, but there was no wolf. This amused the boy, so he did it again. Again, there was no wolf so the people walked away.

NARRATOR: Part e
The boy stood by as he watched the wolf have a meal of his sheep. There was nothing he could do but watch. No one came to help him.

4 Students listen to the story in the correct order to check.

AUDIO SCRIPT

 Track 8.6

There was once a young boy who lived near a dark forest. Every day he had to take care of his sheep. The young boy was lonely and bored.

He decided on a plan to relieve his boredom. He ran into the village shouting, "Wolf! Wolf!" People came to help, but there was no wolf. This amused the boy, so he did it again. Again, there was no wolf, so the people walked away.

Soon after that, a wolf really *did* come into the village and began eyeing his sheep. He was extremely frightened. He cried, "Wolf! Help! This time, there really is a wolf!" The wolf came closer and closer to his sheep.

The boy stood by as he watched the wolf have a meal of his sheep. There was nothing he could do but watch. No one came to help him.

When the boy complained, a wise old man in the village said, "Never lie. Even when a liar tells the truth, no one will believe him."

ANSWERS
1 Exposition   2 Climax   3 Resolution
4 Rising Action   5 Falling Action

E Critical thinking

Applying a framework or model is important in critical thinking. This involves understanding and recognizing basic principles or elements. Recognizing common elements enables comparison and broader, more abstract discussion.

1 Students work in groups to review the stories they made notes on in the *Before you listen* section. The student who made the notes outlines the story, and the other group members help to analyze whether the story follows the five elements.

2 The groups discuss other stories, trying to identify those that do not follow the order of the elements.

PRONUNCIATION

Pronunciation for listening
Emphatic stress for storytelling

Students read through the first part of the *Emphatic stress for storytelling* box. Ask them to then explain which words we tend to emphasize when telling a story in an engaging way (**Possible answer:** *those that give the most unusual, or exciting part of the story*).

Read through the second half of the box with students, modeling the example sentences for them. Ask students to explain the difference in meaning the changing stress brings to the pairs of sentences (**Possible answer:** *in the first sentence, the particular feeling is defined, e.g., being worried, in the second sentence the degree of feeling is emphasized*).

1 Students listen to the sentences and underline the emphasized word.

AUDIO SCRIPT

🎧 **Track 8.7**

1 The *Boy Who Cried Wolf* is a really famous story.
2 The boy was obviously lying to the people in the town.
3 The boy was extremely embarrassed by his actions.
4 The wolf's teeth were enormous!
5 The people in town totally didn't believe the boy.
6 The boy learned a huge lesson that day.

ANSWERS
1 really 2 obviously 3 extremely 4 enormous
5 totally 6 huge

2 Students listen again and then practice saying the sentences with their partners. Monitor and encourage emphatic stress.

3 Students work alone to complete the sentences with an adjective or adverb. Highlight that they should look at the grammar, articles, and meaning of the sentences to decide which word to select for each sentence.

ANSWERS
1 tiny 2 totally 3 long 4 awful 5 Obviously
6 extremely

4 Students work with a partner to say the sentences with the appropriate stress. Monitor and praise use of emphatic stress.

VOCABULARY

Vocabulary development
Descriptive adjectives

Allow time for students to read through the *Descriptive adjectives* box. Demonstrate how to use a thesaurus. This could be a paper copy and / or a high quality online thesaurus such as the *Macmillan Online Dictionary and Thesaurus*.

1 Students work alone to match the words. Allow time for students to compare in pairs, and then check as a class.

ANSWERS
1 e 2 c 3 b 4 f 5 a 6 d

2 Students review the words with a partner. They identify the word which does not fit. Highlight that the other words, while not meaning exactly the same thing, are in the same area of meaning as the first word. If available, students check the answers with a dictionary. Otherwise, check answers as a class.

> **ANSWERS**
> **1** strange **2** plain **3** curious **4** amazing **5** ugly
> **6** loud

3 Students work alone to rewrite the sentences using a word from Exercise 2. They then compare their answers with a partner's.

> **ANSWERS**
> **1** The service at our hotel was awful / horrible / terrible.
> **2** The lion's eyes were massive / enormous / huge.
> **3** A kind / friendly / helpful woman showed me how to find the mall.
> **4** The weather on our trip was excellent / pleasant / great.
> **5** The restaurant served tiny / little / baby-sized food portions.
> **6** We saw one lovely / attractive / beautiful sunset after another.

VOCABULARY ▶

Academic words

1 Students work alone to match the words in bold to the definitions. Allow time for students to compare answers in pairs, and then check as a class.

> **ANSWERS**
> **1** d **2** f **3** c **4** b **5** a **6** g **7** h **8** e

2 Students work in pairs to complete the sentences with words from Exercise 1. Go through the answers with the class.

> **ANSWERS**
> **1** accommodation **2** fee **3** currency **4** tension
> **5** confirmed **6** element **7** drama **8** analysis

3 Students discuss the questions with a partner.

SPEAKING ▶

Speaking model

Warm-up

Have a book race. Write *past progressive*, *words starting or ending with /k/ or /g/*, and *sentence adverbs* as bullet points on the board. Give students one minute to write an example of each (**Possible answers:** *I was waiting for three hours; cat, work, great, dig; obviously*). Then tell students to open their books, check, and complete their answers, calling out when they finish. Check answers and congratulate the winner (i.e., the first to finish).

Read through the aims of the *Speaking* section with students. Remind students that everything they study in this section leads towards the successful completion of the final *Speaking task*.

A Analyze

1 Students read through the story and add the time expressions to the correct place. Check answers as a whole class.

> **ANSWERS**
> **1** a few months ago **2** The week before
> **3** the next day **4** then **5** Finally

2 Students work in pairs to analyze the story in relation to Freytag's Pyramid on page 141. Ask them to analyze and identify each stage of the model in the story.

> **ANSWER**
> No

B Discuss

Students work together to analyze the type of story, and identify any words which indicate the type. They then discuss their views of the story.

GRAMMAR

The past progressive

Read through *The past progressive* box with the students.

1   Students work alone to complete the sentences with the verbs in parentheses in the *past progressive*. Go through the answers with the class.

ANSWERS
1 were climbing   2 was writing   3 were watching
4 was shining, were singing

2   Students work alone to complete the sentences with the correct form of the verbs. Allow time for students to compare answers in pairs, and then check as a class.

ANSWERS
1 were waiting, started   2 got, was sleeping
3 fell, was walking   4 were hurrying, had

3   Students work in pairs to ask and answer the questions. Monitor and help students to reformulate the verbs as necessary.

SPEAKING

Speaking skill
Using sentence adverbs

Give students a few minutes to read through the *Using sentence adverbs* box. Ask students for ideas about how the speaker is feeling for each of the example sentences in the box. Listen, but avoid giving the final answer, as these should become clear through the exercises.

1   Students work alone to match the sentence adverbs to when they are used. Allow time for students to compare in pairs, and then check as a class.

ANSWERS
1 b   2 c   3 a   4 e   5 f   6 d   7 i   8 g   9 h

2   Students work together to select the correct adverb. Go through the answers with the class.

ANSWERS
1 Basically   2 Honestly   3 Thankfully   4 Clearly
5 Luckily

PRONUNCIATION

Pronunciation for speaking
/g/ versus /k/

Read through the /*g*/ versus /*k*/ box with the class. Model the sounds and words. Encourage students to touch their throats as they make the sounds. Because /**g**/ is voiced, vibrations will be felt in the throat, and by the hand when the sound is made. /**k**/ is made in exactly the same way as /**g**/ (i.e., the mouth, lips, and tongue do not move), but it is not voiced, so vibrations will not be felt.

1   Model the activity for the students. Write *gap / cap* on the board, and say one of the words. Students point to the word they hear. Students work in pairs to say one word from the pair, while their partner writes the word they hear.

2   Students review the sentences together and underline the /**g**/ and circle the /**k**/ sounds. Model the sentences for the students for them to check their answers. They then practice the sentences with their partner.

ANSWERS
1 bag   2 called, getting gas   3 counter   4 back, bag
5 book, cab

3   Students listen to part of the story again, underlining the /**g**/ sounds, and circling the /**k**/ sounds. Students then practice reading out the story. As well as focusing on the sounds, they can also focus on the emphatic stress.

ANSWERS

There was once a young boy who lived near a dark forest. Every day he had to take care of his sheep. The young boy was lonely and bored.
He decided on a plan to relieve his boredom. He ran into the village shouting, "Wolf! Wolf!" People came to help but there was no wolf. This amused the boy, so he did it again. Again, there was no wolf, so the people walked away.
Soon after that, a wolf really did come into the village, and began eyeing his sheep. He was extremely frightened. He cried, "Wolf! Help! This time, there really is a wolf!" The wolf came closer and closer to his sheep.

SPEAKING

Speaking task

Brainstorm

1 Students work in pairs to discuss possible stories for each category. Each student should introduce at least one idea for each category, telling the story briefly to their partner.

2 Students work alone to choose a story. They then break it down into parts, making a note of all the key events in order.

Plan

1 Students add the details from Exercise 2 above to the correct part of the Freytag's Pyramid diagram. Ask students to draw a larger version of the diagram, and then add more details about characters, setting, and time.

2 Students explain their diagram to their partner. The partner assesses if the division of the parts is correct, and suggests where more details might make the story more interesting, or clearer.

Speak and share

Students work in groups to tell their stories. As students do this, monitor and note successful and less successful language use in the key areas.

Students then share with their group members what they like about each story, and choose the most interesting. They share the retelling of this story to the whole class.

Have a feedback session on language use. Highlight effective language use you noted, and for less effective use, encourage peer correction, and help the students to reformulate the language.

Reflect

Students share their reflections with a partner. Monitor and join the discussions as appropriate.

REVIEW

Wordlist

Students work in pairs or small groups to work through the *Wordlist*, checking that they all remember what each word or phrase means, how to pronounce it, and how it was used in the unit. Go through the list carefully with the class.

Academic words review

Students work through the sentences, check their answers in pairs, and give feedback to the class.

ANSWERS
1 currency   2 analysis   3 fee   4 recover   5 tension

Unit review

Students work through the list alone to decide what they can and can't do. They discuss their answers in pairs, including what they remember from the unit about each point. Finally, open up the discussion to include the whole class. Pay particular attention to any boxes that the students didn't check. Explore with them ways of overcoming any remaining problems.

Extra research task

As a take-home activity, ask students to research a traditional story from their own country. They make notes on background information (e.g., *history of the story, whether it is told in other countries,* etc.). They should practice telling the story from their notes at home. In the next class, have a presentation of the different stories.

9 ENVIRONMENT

LISTENING 1	Listening for pros and cons
LISTENING 2	Listening to a presenter interact with an audience
STUDY SKILL	Preparing a poster
VOCABULARY	Environment word families
GRAMMAR	Modal passives
SPEAKING	Interacting with a presenter

Warm-up

In the center of the board write *environment*, with three arms coming from the word, labeled *What's in it? What's good for it? What's bad for it?* Elicit an idea for each branch (**Possible answers:** *rivers, local food, cars*). Then ask students to work in pairs to build the mind map. Monitor and ask students to add their ideas to the board. Review the mind map as a whole class when it is complete.

Discussion point

Give students time to read through the infographic. They then discuss the questions in pairs. Invite whole-class feedback on the second question. If there have been changes in use of these things, explore why. Broaden the discussion from a personal to more a general level. Ask questions about general changes in what the public knows about, and what might influence this (e.g., *the media*).

VIDEO

Before you watch

Focus the students on the photo. Elicit what is shown, and encourage the students to guess the difference between the two boxes, using the visual clues to help.

Students work in pairs to match the phrasal verbs to the definitions. Go through the answers with the class.

ANSWERS
1 d 2 c 3 e 4 b 5 a

While you watch

Give students time to read through the statements and predict the answers. Play the video. Students work in pairs to decide if the statements are *T* (True) or *F* (False). Play the audio again as necessary. If statements are false, ask students to correct them. Check answers as a whole class.

ANSWERS
1 F (The Solarbox is green.)   2 T
3 F (Two university graduates from the London School of Economics invented it.)
4 T 5 T

See page 109 for the video script.

After you watch

Students discuss the questions with a partner. When all questions have been discussed, put pairs together, and ask them to share, and expand their list of ideas for question 3. They can categorize their list into *possible now* and *future dream*. Share ideas as a whole class, and build a list of the two categories of ideas on the board.

LISTENING 1

Solar power
A Vocabulary preview

Warm-up

Have an informal debate. In the middle of the board, draw a light bulb. Elicit what it is, and ask all the different ways we can make electricity to turn it on (**Possible answers:** *using gas, oil, nuclear, solar power, wind*). Write the students' ideas on the board around the light bulb. Ask students to choose a form of power, but not *solar power*. They should then work in pairs to brainstorm a list of pros and cons for the form of energy they chose. Monitor and encourage students to think freely, and generate several ideas. They then review their ideas and prioritize them. Put pairs together with another pair that has focused on the same energy source. Ask them to have a debate. Ask a student to explain how a debate works, or explain yourself, as necessary. Assign sides to one student from each pair, and set a time limit for the debate. The other two students watch the debate and vote at the end.

1. Students work alone to match the words to the definitions. Allow time for students to compare in pairs, and then check with the class. Establish the word stress when checking, and model, and drill the language with the class.

> ANSWERS
>
> **1** f **2** e **3** g **4** b **5** a **6** d **7** h **8** c

2. Students work alone to complete the sentences with the words from Exercise 1. Go through the answers with the class.

> ANSWERS
>
> **1** fuel **2** dishwasher **3** solar, store
> **4** supply, renewable **5** install, panels

3. Students review the sentences, making a note of those they agree with. Then students share and discuss their choices with a partner.

B Before you listen

Activating prior knowledge

Elicit the students' understanding of the term *environmentally friendly*. Then students work in pairs or small groups to discuss each type of energy in relation to the question. Monitor and encourage the students to use the *Why?* prompt to extend their discussion.

C Global listening

Listening for main ideas

Allow time for students to review the questions. Ask them to identify the key words in the questions (**Possible answer:** *the question word plus the key vocabulary words, e.g., Why / talking / solar*). Play the audio. Students compare their answers with a partner. Go through the answers with the class.

> AUDIO SCRIPT
>
> **Track 9.1**
>
> **AICHA:** Hi Steven.
>
> **STEVEN:** Oh, hi, Aicha. I'm glad you could make it.
>
> **AICHA:** Well, our class debate is tomorrow. It's really important that we practice.
>
> **STEVEN:** I know. We need to be prepared if we're going to do well. Did you make some notes?
>
> **AICHA:** Yes, I found some interesting stuff on the Internet. There is so much out there on solar energy.
>
> **STEVEN:** I know! So ... we both researched the pros and cons of solar power. We should be prepared to talk about either side, right? Do you want to talk about the pros, and I'll talk about the cons? That's how our debate will probably go. We won't know which side we'll have to argue for.

> **AICHA:** OK. Well, I feel that converting sunlight into energy is the answer to most of our energy problems. Solar energy is the future. And I know at least several reasons we should use it more. First, solar energy is renewable. That means we will always have it, unlike fuels like oil and gas. It is estimated oil and gas will only last another 60 years. The sun could be used forever, or at least another 6.5 billion years.
>
> **STEVEN:** Yes, the sun will always supply us with light, but solar power is not always available because the sun doesn't shine at night, or when it's cloudy. And some places get very little sun in the winter, like Norway, Sweden, or Russia. There may be only seven hours of sunlight a day, or less.
>
> **AICHA:** But, you have the capacity to store solar energy. You just need batteries.
>
> **STEVEN:** True, but the batteries are large and heavy. They are the size of a dishwasher or small washing machine, weigh up to 120 kilograms and can easily cost over $5,000. Another problem with solar energy is that it's not very effective when there is air pollution, like in large cities. Even if it's sunny, solar energy won't be effective.
>
> **AICHA:** OK, but another good thing about solar energy is that it can get to many places—places that currently don't have electricity. That helps a lot of people. And of course, it's environmentally friendly and does not cause pollution.
>
> **STEVEN:** But there can be pollution caused by building and moving solar power systems.
>
> **AICHA:** But it's not a lot. After you install solar panels, for example, they are 100% clean. Another big reason we should use solar energy is that it reduces our electricity costs. People can even sell any extra energy they produce. I came across some data online that is very relevant to this issue. It said a lot of money could be saved by adding solar panels to your home. You can save up to $100 dollars a month. In places like the U.S state of Hawaii, residents would save on average $64,000 in just 20 years! That's huge.
>
> **STEVEN:** But remember the initial costs of buying and setting up solar panels are high.
>
> **AICHA:** But they are getting cheaper. In the last ten years the cost of roof panels has declined 80%. And you only need to clean them once or twice a year. They don't have moving parts and can last for about 25 years. It's smart to invest in them.
>
> **STEVEN:** But a large amount of space may be needed. That might not be an issue for a family in a home—panels can be placed on the roof. But it's a definite problem for some businesses, which may need to find space for hundreds of panels. OK, I'll give you the last word.
>
> **AICHA:** Well, the last point I want to make is that solar energy is quiet. There is no noise, unlike wind energy.
>
> **STEVEN:** Good point. So, are we prepared for tomorrow?
>
> **AICHA:** I think so. But why don't we practice one more time. Let's take opposite roles ...

D Close listening

Listening for pros and cons

Ask students about how Aicha and Steven prepared for the debate (**Answer:** *they thought about both the pros and cons of an issue*). Elicit comments on how this helped students to prepare. Then open books, and read through the *Close listening* box with the students.

Exam skill

Writing and speaking tasks in exams such as IELTS often involve coming to a conclusion on an issue. In a writing task, this may be structured as an advantages / disadvantages essay. However, if there is no formal structure for this in the task, it is good to show that you are able to consider both sides of an argument. Being able to discuss (and refute) an opposing argument often strengthens the actual view being put forward.

Allow time for students to review the notes to be completed. Play the audio. Allow time for students to note their answers, and then compare them with a partner. Play the audio again as required, dividing it into parts, and giving time for students to discuss, and confirm their answers after each part. Go through the answers with the class.

ANSWERS

Pros: 2 batteries **4** clean **5** sell **6** cheaper **7** quiet
Cons: 2 expensive **4** building **5** high **6** space

AUDIO SCRIPT

🎧 **Track 9.1**

E Critical thinking

Considering all sides of an issue before deciding if it is positive or negative is a key element of critical thinking. This can be done in a more formal way, as with the notes on pros and cons in the *Close listening* section, but also more informally. Encouraging students to develop this habit will strengthen their critical thinking skills.

Allow time for students to review the notes in the *Close listening* section. Then students discuss the questions in small groups. Students report the key points of their discussion to the class. Encourage other students to respond to these when listening in whole-class feedback.

STUDY SKILLS

Preparing a poster

Warm-up

Ask students to close their eyes. Tell them to imagine a poster which gives information about the pros and cons of wind power. Ask students to call out what they can see (in their mind's eye) on the poster (**Possible answers:** *titles, writing, pictures, color, bullet points*). For each idea ask questions (e.g., *How big is the writing? What is in the picture?*). Add the students' ideas to the board. Then ask students to open their eyes and continue the discussion. Ask *What makes a good information poster? What makes a bad information poster?* Then ask students to open books and review the *Preparing a poster* box.

Students read through the information in the *Study skills* box. For each point, ask how the viewer would feel if the poster didn't have these features (i.e., if it wasn't *large, bright, and informative*).

1   Students brainstorm other features that good posters have in pairs. Share answers as a whole class.

2   Students work in pairs to review the poster, making suggestions for changes, and additions to improve the poster. Then put pairs together to compare their analysis of the poster.

Extension activity

If the Internet is available, students review examples of posters for presentations online. Ask students to evaluate examples using the criteria established in the *Study skills* box, and in Exercise 2. Students present good and less good examples to the class, outlining their evaluation of these posters.

LISTENING 2

Eco-tourism

A Vocabulary preview

1   Students work alone to match the words in bold to the definitions. Allow time for students to compare in pairs, and then check as a class.

ANSWERS

1 f **2** e **3** a **4** h **5** d **6** g **7** b **8** c

2   Ask students to identify the vocabulary words from Exercise 1 in the questions (**Answer:** *tourism, preserve, remote, sensitive, beneficial*). Students then discuss the questions in pairs. When all the questions have been

discussed, change pairs, and ask students to report their discussion to their new partner, and identify any similarities in views.

B Before you listen

Activating prior knowledge

Students review the activities alone. Clarify the meaning of vocabulary as necessary (though avoid focusing on *eco-friendly* and the question it is in). Once they have ranked them, students compare their order with a partner. Ask them to discuss why they made these choices.

Clarify the concept of *eco-friendly*, and ask students to assess how eco-friendly each activity is. Put pairs together to share ideas, and see how much they agree.

C Global listening

Listening to order information

1   Allow time for students to review the poster. Encourage them to comment on the elements, assessing what is effective about it (e.g., *the colorful pictures*). Play the audio, and students number the parts of the poster in the order they are presented.

AUDIO SCRIPT

 Track 9.2

PRESENTER: Hello. Can I tell you a little bit about my poster? It's on the topic of tourism.

LISTENER 1:   Sure!

PRESENTER: First, I think it's important to answer the question: What is eco-tourism? The World Tourism Forum defines eco-tourism as tourism that sends people to mostly untouched parts of the world, and that is sensitive to the impact on nature caused by humans. Its aim is to show that tourism does not need to harm nature or traditional culture. It's an idea that appeals to people who want to travel to these places, but want to do it in an environmentally friendly way.

LISTENER 1:   Sounds great.

PRESENTER: It's the fastest-growing type of tourism. It grows between 10 and 15% every year. To say a bit more about that, it's been growing like that since the 1980s, and it's not slowing down. So I think we can say that eco-tourism is here to stay.

PRESENTER: But is it a good thing?

PRESENTER: Let's look at the pros. It helps preserve nature. The preservation of our land, forests, lakes, and oceans is very important. It uses local resources to build with, and local food to feed tourists. It doesn't waste electricity or water. In fact, water is often rainwater, and no electricity may be used at all.

PRESENTER: It also creates jobs, and income, for locals. Any money or fees that tourists pay goes back into the community. Local people are more likely to protect wildlife, too.

LISTENER 1:   Can you talk a little more about that?

PRESENTER: Sure. Show an elephant living in the forest to tourists, rather than bringing the elephant out of that environment.

PRESENTER: Eco-tourism can allow us to see more of the world and its cultures. This is good for people who are in urban environments as well as rural. Both sides can learn from each other.

PRESENTER: What I'd like to mention now is the Arabian oryx, in Jordan. This is a photo here. It's a beautiful animal. By 1920, they had all died out. In 1978, Jordan reintroduced 11 of the animals to the country. They were placed in protected areas, and now there are over 200. Tourists can now see these animals on guided tours. The money from these tours helps protect the oryx.

While there are good things about eco-tourism, there are also some negative things. It has the potential to damage nature. Tourists may do this by accident, but it happens. An example is that of Africa, where many people go on safari to see wild animals. Vehicles full of tourists drive out to see animals in the morning, when it's cooler. They scare off animals that lions are trying to catch. This means that lions cannot find food in the morning. They have to look for food in the afternoon, when it's hot.

LISTENER 2:   Sorry, but can I ask a question? Why is that so bad?

PRESENTER: When it's that hot out, the animals have less energy, so it's harder to find food.

Also, there is little control over eco-tourism because many tours go to remote places. There's nothing stopping people from taking money from tourists, or not following eco-friendly practices. Just because someone says they are eco-friendly is no guarantee that it is true.

And finally, eco-tourism changes cultures, even when we don't want it to.

LISTENER 2:   What do you mean by that?

PRESENTER: Take the Maasai people for instance. Here they are in this photo. Tourists pay money to see them dance. As a result, they no longer follow their own traditions as much. Sadly, tourists are destroying the cultures they think they are helping. It has happened in the Amazon, Africa, Southeast Asia, Greenland, the Andes—all over the world.

Now look here. That's me. As you can see in this photo, I was part of a snorkeling tour. It was advertised as an eco-tour. A group of us went snorkeling to see and photograph the coral. Then I saw people standing on the coral. It was awful. That's why I want to end with some tips. If you decide you want to go on an eco-tour, keep these tips in mind.

1 Don't accept everything you hear or read. Many tour companies only use terms like "eco" and "green" to attract people.

2 Search for reviews of companies online. That's what I do.

3 Check the group size. Imagine the harm a group of 35 can do versus a group of four.

4 Make sure companies follow the rules of eco-tourism. Ask lots of questions.

5 Make sure local people benefit. But remember this: buying a local product from a store may not be enough. See if the money goes directly to helping local communities.

6 Make sure the accommodation is built from renewable materials. Renewable materials are natural materials; for example, wood, stone, bamboo, and grass.

To conclude, I'm happy to send you a link to a list of eco-tours that I would recommend.

ANSWERS
1 the title (Eco-tourism)
2 the definition (Eco-tourism is …)
3 the aims (It aims …)
4 the pros (The good)
5 the animal picture
6 the cons (The bad)
7 the dancers picture
8 the snorkeling picture
9 the tips

---

2 Students discuss the best subtitle. Go through the answers with the class.

ANSWER
c

D Close listening

Listening to a presenter interact with the audience

With books closed, ask students *who* spoke during the listening (**Answer:** *the presenter plus two people from the audience*). Ask if they thought the presenter was happy to interact with the people (**Answer:** *yes, she agreed to it, gave full answers, and didn't tell people to stop asking questions*).

Give students time to read through the *Listening to a presenter interact with the audience* box. Check understanding. Then give them a few minutes to study the information in more detail, focusing on the phrases used. Ask students to close their books, and elicit phrases from students, building them up on the board.

1 Read through the task with students. Then play the excerpts, and students number them in order.

AUDIO SCRIPT

🎧 **Track 9.3**

1

PRESENTER: Hello. Can I tell you a little bit about my poster? It's on the topic of tourism.

2

PRESENTER: It's the fastest-growing type of tourism. It grows between 10 and 15% every year. To say a bit more about that, it's been growing like that since the 1980s, and it's not slowing down.

3

PRESENTER: As you can see in this photo, I was part of a snorkeling tour. It was advertised as an eco-tour.

4

PRESENTER: To conclude, I'm happy to send you a link to a list of eco-tours that I would recommend.

ANSWERS
1 She invites someone to listen.
2 She further explains an idea.
3 She refers to a visual.
4 She offers additional information.

---

2 Give students time to review the tips, and the way the presenter expands on them. Then play the excerpt. Students then match the items, compare their answers with a partner's, and then check as a class.

AUDIO SCRIPT

 Track 9.4

PRESENTER: If you decide you want to go on an eco-tour, keep these tips in mind.

1 Don't accept everything you hear or read. Many tour companies only use terms like "eco" and "green" to attract people.

2 Search for reviews of companies online. That's what I do.

3 Check the group size. Imagine the harm a group of 35 can do versus a group of four.

4 Make sure companies follow the rules of ecotourism. Ask lots of questions.

5 Make sure local people benefit. But remember this: buying a local product from a store may not be enough. See if the money goes directly to helping local communities.

6 Make sure the accommodation is built from renewable materials. Renewable materials are natural materials; for example, wood, stone, bamboo, and grass.

ANSWERS

1 a **2** d **3** e **4** c **5** f **6** b

E Critical thinking

Students develop the skill of weighing evidence in order to come to a final decision. This is an important skill for making complex, and often important decisions.

Ask students to review the pros and cons of eco-tourism. In small groups, they complete a column for each, drawing on the information learned through the listening. Then mix up the groups, and ask students to compare and add to their columns if necessary. Then students discuss eco-tourism, attempting to come to a group decision on whether the pros outweigh the cons. Once the decisions have been made, open up the discussion to the whole class.

Students discuss the questions they would ask an eco-tour company. Share ideas as a whole class.

Extension activity

Create a list of FAQs. Clarify the term *FAQ* (*Frequently Asked Questions*). Students work in small groups to write a list of questions they would want an eco-tour company to answer if they were thinking of joining them on a tour. Students then exchange the list with another group. They now imagine they are the ecotourism company answering the new list of FAQs for their website. When the answers are written, groups post the FAQs and answers on the wall of the class. Students review all the company FAQs, and decide which company they will use for their eco-tour.

Pronunciation for listening
Linking vowel sounds between words

Allow time for students to read through the *Linking vowel sounds between words* box in pairs. Ask them to check understanding with each other. As they do this, write some examples from the box on the board, but without marking the linking sound. With books closed, ask students to explain the main ideas from the box, and to identify the linking sounds in the examples. Students then review the box to check. Demonstrate the mouth movement as described in the skills box, exaggerating for students to see. Ask them to practice the examples with a partner, exaggerating and noticing the mouth movements. Make sure students understand using linking sounds is natural and happens in order to make the transition between words smoother.

1 Students review the sentences in pairs, and predict the linking sound. Then play the audio while they listen and check their predictions. They then practice the sentences, listening to, and giving feedback to their partner.

ANSWERS

1 /j/ **2** /w/ **3** /j/ **4** /w/ **5** /j/ **6** /j/ **7** /w/ **8** /w/

AUDIO SCRIPT

 Track 9.5

1 It's really important that we practice.

2 That's how our debate will probably go.

3 Solar energy is the future.

4 And I know at least several reasons we should use it more.

5 There may be only seven hours of sunlight a day.

6 They are the size of a dishwasher or a small washing machine.

7 You can save up to a hundred dollars a month.

8 So are we prepared for tomorrow?

2 Students work alone to identify where the linking sound is. Then ask them to compare in pairs. Go through the answers with the class. Then have students practice saying the sentences with their partner.

ANSWERS

1 you a /w/ **2** money or /j/ **3** allow us /w/
4 who are /w/ **5** go on /w/ **6** see if /j/

VOCABULARY

Vocabulary development
Environment word families

With books closed, on the board write *advertisement, protection, argument,* and *installation.* Elicit the type of word (**Answer:** *noun*), and ask what the words have in common. Students may focus on the meaning, so direct them to looking at the form of the word (**Answer:** *they all have suffixes*). Ask students to identify the words with the suffixes removed, and elicit the word type (**Answer:** *advertise, protect, argue, install—verbs*). Open books, and read through the box with the students.

1   Students work with a partner to complete the chart. If available, students use a dictionary to check. Go through the answers with the class.

> **ANSWERS**
> 1 attract—attraction   2 conserve—conservation
> 3 damage—damage   4 develop—development
> 5 install—installation   6 question—question
> 7 pollute—pollution   8 power—power
> 9 preserve —preservation   10 produce—production
> 11 supply—supply

Extension activity

Tell students they are going to look at changing word stress (there is a more in-depth focus on this area in *Pronunciation for speaking,* later in the unit). Ask students to identify the word stress pattern in each verb and noun. They will notice that the stress shifts from the first to the second syllable with the word *produce.* This is a common stress shift for words which are both verbs and nouns (e.g., *import, export, record*). However, note, this does not happen with the other verb-nouns in Exercise 1 (e.g., *damage, question, power, supply*). Students will also notice that the stress shifts with the addition of *–ation* (e.g., *conserve o O—conservation o o O o*). Model and drill the words with students.

2   Students work alone to complete the questions with the words from Exercise 1. Go through the answers with the class.

> **ANSWERS**
> 1 pollution   2 argument   3 power   4 conserve
> 5 attract   6 develop / produce   7 damage

3   Students ask and answer the questions from Exercise 2. Monitor, noticing and praising the correct use and pronunciation of the key words.

VOCABULARY

Academic words

1   Students work alone to match the words in bold to the definitions. Ask students to check their answers in pairs, and then check as a class.

> **ANSWERS**
> 1 d   2 c   3 e   4 a   5 f   6 h   7 b   8 g

2   Students work alone to complete the sentences with the words from Exercise 1. Go through the answers with the class.

> **ANSWERS**
> 1 definite   2 potential   3 relevant   4 capacity
> 5 fees   6 convert   7 guarantee   8 data

3   Students discuss the questions in pairs or small groups. Encourage them to support their views and to focus on those statements they disagree on. Ask students to report to the class on the statements which created the most interesting discussion.

SPEAKING

Speaking model

Read through the aims of the *Speaking* section with the students. Remind them that all the work done in this section leads to the successful completion of the final task. Elicit what the final task is (**Answer:** *to conduct a poster presentation*), and remind students of the work they have already done on this in the *Study Skills* section of the unit.

A Analyze

1   Read the task instructions with students. Then students read the model, and complete it with the phrases. Go through the answers with the class.

> **ANSWERS**
> 1 Would you like to hear about wind power   2 As you see here on this poster   3 Notice in this picture that
> 4 Let me just add that   5 I'm happy to send you a link

2   Students identify the words used to move to the next part of the presentation.

> **ANSWERS**
> First, Second, Finally, Also, Another

B Discuss

Students discuss the questions in pairs or small groups. They need to be able to see both the poster on page 157 and the model as they do this. Monitor and encourage analysis of the poster, prompting students with further questions. Share main points of the discussion as a whole class.

GRAMMAR >

Modal passives

Ask students to close their books, and on the board write *Solar panels can be placed on the roof.* Elicit the meaning of the sentence from students. Ask *Do we know who can place the panels on the roof?* (**Answer:** *no*); *Which roof?* (**Answer:** *we don't know, and it's not important*). Elicit the names of the parts of the form (**Answers:** *modal, be, past participle*). Open books, and ask students to tell you the name of the grammatical form (**Answer:** *modal passives*).

Allow time for students to read through the *Modal passives* box. Ask them to underline the modal passives in the example sentences.

1   Students work alone to complete the sentences with the modal passive form, using the verb in parentheses. Ask students to check in pairs, and then check as a class.

ANSWERS
1 be finished   2 be found   3 be taught   4 be sold
5 be saved   6 be replaced

---

2   Read through the example sentence with students, highlighting how the two sentences essentially have the same meaning, but the focus is different. Ask what the focus is on in the second sentence (**Answer:** *the food*). Ask if we are interested in who is, or may be wasting it (**Answer:** *no*). Students work in pairs to transform the sentences. Go through the answers with the class.

ANSWERS
1 The rules in the national park have to be followed.
2 Great eco-tourism deals can be found online.
3 Computers should be put to sleep at night.
4 The eco-tour can't be paid for with a credit card.

---

3   Ask students to identify the modal passive forms in the two questions (**Answer:** *Should ... be required ...* and *... needs to be done*). Students then discuss the questions in pairs or small groups. During whole-class feedback, build a list of suggestions for question 2 on the board. Review the list as a class, and identify those which are likely to happen, and those which aren't.

SPEAKING >

Speaking skill
Interacting with a presenter

Allow time for students to read through the *Interacting with a presenter* box. Model and drill the example sentences and questions. Students can highlight the main stresses on the phrases.

1   Students work in pairs to match the two parts of the sentences and questions. Go through the answers with the class. Then allow time for students to practice the phrases in pairs.

ANSWERS
1 e   2 a   3 d   4 b   5 g   6 c   7 h   8 f

---

2   Read through the task instructions with students. Play the audio. Then students compare their answers with a partner's. Play the audio again as required.

AUDIO SCRIPT

🎧 **Track 9.6**

1

PRESENTER: It's an idea that appeals to people who want to travel to these places, but want to do it in an environmentally friendly way.

LISTENER 1:   Sounds great.

PRESENTER: It's the fastest-growing type of tourism. It grows between 10 and 15% every year.

2

PRESENTER: Local people are more likely to protect wildlife, too.

LISTENER 1:   Can you talk a little more about that?

PRESENTER: Sure. Show an elephant living in the forest to tourists, rather than bringing the elephant out of that environment.

3

PRESENTER: They scare off animals that lions are trying to catch. This means that lions cannot find food in the morning. They have to look for food in the afternoon, when it's hot.

LISTENER 2:   Sorry, but can I ask a question? Why is that so bad?

PRESENTER: When it's that hot out, the animals have less energy, so it's harder to find food.

4

PRESENTER: And finally, eco-tourism changes cultures, even when we don't want it to.

LISTENER 2:   What do you mean by that?

PRESENTER: Take the Maasai people in East Africa, for instance.

---

3 Read through the instructions with students. Elicit what each student in the pair is going to do. As the student talks, monitor and make a note of effective and less effective language use in the area of the phrases (and modal passives).

4 Students change roles. Again, monitor and make a note of language use. Have whole-class feedback focusing on the notes you made while monitoring. Praise effective language use, and help the students to reformulate less effective use.

PRONUNCIATION ⟩

Pronunciation for speaking
Word stress with word suffixes

Students read through the *Word stress with word suffixes* box. Encourage them to say the example words in the box, focusing on the correct positioning of the stress. Monitor and assist as required.

1 Students work in pairs to identify the stress in the words in first column only. Monitor and assist by modeling the correct stress. Go through the answers with the class.

2 Students work in the same pairs to identify the stress in the words in the second column. Tell them there is only one word in which the stress does not move (**Answer:** *eLECtric / eLECtrical*). Do not monitor or assist during this exercise.

3 Play the audio for students to listen and check. Allow time for students to practice saying the words with their partner.

AUDIO SCRIPT

🎧 **Track 9.7**

1 benefit, beneficial
2 install, installation
3 preserve, preservation
4 electric, electrical
5 present, presentation
6 inform, information
7 prepare, preparation
8 environment, environmentally

4 Students review the sentences, marking the stress in the key words. Then they practice saying the sentences with their partner. Monitor, assist, and model as required.

SPEAKING ⟩

Speaking task

Read the task with the students. Then allow time for students to look back through the unit to identify parts which will be useful for the task.

Brainstorm and plan

1 Students work in pairs and establish which student is A and which is B.

2 Students work alone to review their partner's poster and write the three questions.

Students then work alone to analyze their own poster, deciding on the order to present the information. The students should make notes on what they will say, using the three points in the book as guidance.

Speak and share

Students give their poster presentations, and respond to questions from their partner. Monitor and make notes of effective and less effective language use.

Students then discuss their presentations, and give feedback to their partners about what was successful in their presentations.

Have a feedback session on language use. Share the examples you noted, and highlight effective language use. For less successful language use, encourage peer correction, and help the students to reformulate the language.

Reflect

Students reflect on the questions individually. Ask them to make a note of their reflections, and to share their ideas with their partner for doing things differently next time.

Wordlist

Students work in pairs or small groups to work through the *Wordlist*, checking that they all remember what each word or phrase means, how to pronounce it, and how it was used in the unit. Go through the list carefully with the class.

Academic words review

Students work through the sentences. Ask students to check their answers in pairs, and then check as a class.

> **ANSWERS**
> **1** potential **2** convert **3** data **4** capacity **5** affect

Unit review

Students work through the list alone to decide what they can and can't do. They discuss their answers in pairs, including what they remember from the unit about each point. Finally, open up the discussion to include the whole class. Pay particular attention to any boxes that the students didn't check. Explore with them ways of overcoming any remaining problems.

Extra research task

As a take-home activity, ask students to research an environmentally friendly project or law that they think will have a positive effect. They can prepare a poster in groups, and present the information to the class in the next lesson.

10 MEDICINE

LISTENING 1	Listening to how an argument is supported
LISTENING 2	Listening for speaker attitude
STUDY SKILL	Persuading through reasons
VOCABULARY	Medical vocabulary
GRAMMAR	Indirect questions
SPEAKING	Refuting an argument

Warm-up

Write *Medicine* on the board, and ask students to call out any related words they know. Add them in a random order to the board. (This could be anything related to the body, medicine, doctors, etc. You decide what is useful to write on the board.) When finished, review the words as a class. Check the meaning of the words, asking the student who suggested the word to define its meaning. Identify any categories (e.g., *the body, disease, technology*) that are evident. Establish the headings for these categories. Then students work in pairs to categorize all the words.

Discussion point

Students read through the infographic. Ask them to make a note of any words they are not sure of. Then put the students in small groups, and ask them to discuss the meaning of unknown words. Monitor and assist as necessary. Clarify as a whole class any words which several groups have on their lists.

Students discuss question 1. Remind them they need to make two decisions for each focus in the infographic, one from a doctor's perspective, and one from a patient's perspective. Monitor and encourage discussion. As whole-class feedback, list the six technological developments on the board with a column for *patients* and a column for *doctors*. Keep a tally of students' views on which they would like to use from each perspective. Review the data as a whole class to identify the most popular and least popular choices. Ask for students' comments (e.g., *What is the most surprising result? Why?*).

Students discuss the other two questions. Again, monitor and supply vocabulary as required. Share main ideas as a whole class.

VIDEO

Before you watch

Focus the students on the picture and ask them to tell you what they can see (**Possible answers:** *spade, digging, grass, dirt*). Ask students *Why do people dig?* Encourage student suggestions, including more creative ideas (**Possible answers:** *to plant seeds, to bury things*).

Students then work alone to match the words to the definitions. Go through the answers with the class.

> ANSWERS
> **1** e **2** b **3** a **4** d **5** c

While you watch

Allow time for students to review the questions and answer options. Then play the video. Students answer the questions and then check their answers with a partner's. Play the video again as required.

> ANSWERS
> **1** a **2** b **3** a

See page 109 for the video script.

After you watch

Students discuss the questions in pairs. After all the questions have been discussed, put pairs together to share ideas and views. Elicit key ideas from the groups as whole-class feedback.

LISTENING 1

Face-to-face vs. online doctors

A Vocabulary preview

1 Students work alone to match the words in bold to the definitions. Allow time for students to compare their answers in pairs, and then check as a class.

> ANSWERS
> **1** e **2** a **3** g **4** b **5** c **6** f **7** h **8** d

2   Students work alone to complete the sentences with the words from Exercise 1. Go through the answers with the class.

ANSWERS

1 prescription   **2** upload   **3** concern   **4** persuade
5 abuse   **6** matter   **7** convenient   **8** rely on

---

3   Allow time for students to review the sentences alone, making a note of opinions. Students then share and discuss their opinion with a partner. Ask pairs to report on the sentences they most agreed with, and those they most disagreed with in whole-class feedback.

B   Before you listen

Activating prior knowledge

1   On the board, write *Seeing the doctor*. Then ask for student suggestions as to what people think about when going to see a doctor (e.g., *cost, time, location, reputation of doctor*), and list them on the board. Students then focus on the task, deciding which of the topics on the board are relevant to the two different types of doctor visits (i.e., *online* and *face-to-face*). Ask if they can think of other relevant topics.

2   Students discuss the questions in pairs. Ask students to identify similarities as well as differences for the first question. In whole-class feedback, have a show of hands to see which type of doctor is more popular with the class.

C   Global listening

Listening for the order of events

1   Allow time for students to review the topics, and check the meaning of vocabulary as necessary. Ask them to identify words from the *Vocabulary preview* section (**Answer:** *abuse, convenience (convenient), prescription*). Play the audio. Students number the topics, and then go through the answers with the class.

AUDIO SCRIPT

🎧 Track 10.1

SONIA: So our debate topic is face-to-face doctors versus online doctors.

MICHAEL: George and I will argue that seeing a doctor face to face is better than seeing a doctor online.

GEORGE: We feel we have many strong reasons that can support our claim.

SONIA: And we'll make an argument for the opposite …

CLARICE: … that these days seeing a doctor online, or using the Internet, is preferable to seeing one face to face. We're sure we can persuade you with our arguments. Do you want to go first?

MICHAEL: Sure, thank you. First, it's common knowledge that the only way for a doctor to find out what is wrong is through a face-to-face meeting. A mistake is more likely to occur when the doctor is only examining you over a video.

SONIA: I don't think that's really true. We believe that an online doctor can see what is wrong with a patient. Not all illnesses of course, but many.

CLARICE: And think about how convenient an online doctor can be for a patient. People are busy these days. With online doctors, they can just send in the information they want. For example, you can send in an image of a skin cut, or upload a blood pressure record. This might save you a visit to the doctor's office altogether.

GEORGE: It's true that it can be more convenient, but it's also more dangerous. The doctor could give a patient the wrong medicine. Everyone knows that it's extremely dangerous to write a prescription for any medicine online. This can only be done safely and responsibly through a face-to-face visit.

SONIA: But online you have access to more doctors, because you can see any doctor, even one in another country. You don't have that option with face-to-face doctors. And increased access also means more people can get medical care. Those who live in remote areas may not get the care they need because they don't live near a big hospital or clinic.

MICHAEL: But you still don't have the personal experience of a face-to-face doctor. That matters a lot. A patient-doctor relationship is built on closeness and trust. It's impossible to develop that online.

SONIA: I'm afraid that's not accurate. It's not easy, but it is possible. It just takes more time. And I'm not sure patients care about that as much as you think. Do you know what percentage of people are happy to see online doctors? One recent statistic showed that nearly two-thirds of patients in the United States said they would see a doctor online.

CLARICE: Seeing a doctor online also means you can get a second opinion more easily. Do you know what a second opinion is?

MICHAEL: It's when you ask another doctor for his opinion, rather than relying on a single doctor's opinion.

CLARICE: Exactly. It's a fact that these days many insurance companies require patients to get a second opinion. And many patients want a second opinion before they make a major medical decision. This is simple to do online because doctors can share the patient's medical history easily.

GEORGE: That may be true, but that's a big concern. What about a patient's privacy? One researcher found that people are becoming more and more worried about their personal information being shared digitally. No one wants that information to be shared with anyone who is not their own doctor. People have real concerns about privacy these days.

MICHAEL: Another issue is the abuse that can take place online.

SONIA: What do you mean "abuse"?

MICHAEL: Abuse of the medical system. Some people may try to use online doctors to get medicine that they want, but don't need. Only with a personal face-to-face meeting can a doctor determine if a patient needs a certain medicine. Experts say that abuse of the medical system is rising, and it could become an even more serious problem.

CLARICE: That's not fair to say. There is no evidence that this "abuse" only takes place with online doctors. We feel the main reason seeing an online doctor is better than a face-to-face doctor is a simple one: it costs less. Let me give you an example. A face-to-face meeting may cost between $130 and $180, but only $40 to $70 online. That's a huge difference.

GEORGE: You claim that online doctors can save patients money. But what good is the cost savings if you don't get what you want? You might waste your money—and time—with an online doctor if you need to go see a doctor face to face after that anyway. You're spending more money.

SONIA: Hmm. I don't know about that. I feel that …

ANSWERS

1 accuracy of doctor's assessment
2 convenience of getting medical care
3 giving a prescription for medicine
4 access to medical care
5 how personal the experience is
6 getting a second opinion from another doctor
7 patient privacy
8 abuse of the healthcare system
9 cost of medical care
Not discussed: dependence on technology

---

2 Students identify the topics which they had discussed in the *Before you listen* section.

3 Discuss the question as a whole class. Ask for students to provide support for their view, and encourage cross-class discussion.

D Close listening
Listening to how an argument is supported

Allow time for students to read through the *Listening to how an argument is supported* box and study the phrases. Then with books closed, write up the four categories from the box (i.e., *Common sense*, etc.). Ask students to recall the phrases, and build them up on the board. Students then open their books to check.

Read through the task with the students, and highlight the letters used for each category. Students also review the arguments 1–6. Then play the audio. Students compare answers. Play the audio again as required, and check answers with the class.

AUDIO SCRIPT

 Track 10.1

ANSWERS
1 CS 2 CS 3 FS 4 EO 5 EO 6 ED

E Critical thinking

Recognizing arguments and evaluating their strength is an important part of critical thinking. Using a conscious process helps to develop skills in this area. Here, the students have just identified the types of arguments. Now they will evaluate them.

Highlight to students the difference between questions 1 and 2. Question 1 focuses on the students' view of the arguments, rather than their view of types of doctors. Question 2 is about their own opinion of types of doctors. This is an important distinction to make. Highlight that people often participate in debates arguing for a view which they do not personally believe in.

The evaluation of the arguments may not alter their final view on which type of doctor is better, online or face-to-face doctors. However, it will mean their view is more informed, and better able to be supported.

Students discuss the questions in small groups. Monitor and encourage the sharing of ideas. Invite whole-class feedback, highlighting that students are focusing on the strength of the arguments put forward in the audio, rather than on their own personal views.

Students make a final decision. Conduct a whole-class vote, and then a show of hands as to student opinion before starting on this unit. Comment on any changes.

Argument: persuasion through reasons

Warm-up

With books closed, describe a person you know who is very good at arguing (i.e., they are persuasive and convincing). This could be in an academic or personal context. Ask students to describe a similar person they know to their partner. Then ask the pairs to identify the elements of the person's arguments, and the skills that help the person to be persuasive (e.g., *they always have lots of evidence to support their view*). Share ideas as a whole class.

Allow time for students to read through the *Argument: persuasion through reasons* box, and check understanding of it with a partner.

1 In pairs, students discuss the positions and match them to the persuasive sentences. Go through the answers with the class.

> ANSWERS
> **1** b **2** c **3** a

2 Allow time for students to read through the text. They then discuss the questions with a partner.

> ANSWERS
> 1 To persuade the reader that natural treatments are not always better.
> 2 Modern medicine is better than natural treatments.
> 3 To accept the scientific evidence for modern medicine's effectiveness.
> 4 Diseases such as polio and small pox have been cured by modern medicine.

LISTENING 2 >

Medical tourism

A Vocabulary preview

1 Students work alone to match the words in bold to the definitions. Allow time for students to compare their answers with a partner's before going through the answers with the class.

> ANSWERS
> **1** a **2** e **3** h **4** d **5** g **6** b **7** c **8** f

2 Allow time for students to review the sentences, deciding which they disagree with or think are false. Students then compare their views with a partner's. Students report back to the class on those statements they had different views on. Encourage whole-class discussion.

B Before you listen

Activating prior knowledge

If you are from a different country than your students, describe the medical care system in your country: talk about *the system, the cost, the provision*, etc. Students then discuss the questions with a partner. During whole-class feedback, ask for a show of hands on how many students would consider going overseas for medical treatment. Elicit a few key reasons why they would or wouldn't do this.

C Global listening

Listening to order information

Allow time for the students to review the slides for the webinar. Check vocabulary as required (e.g., *malpractice—careless or criminal behavior by someone with an official job*). Establish the task, and then play the audio. Go through the answers with the class.

AUDIO SCRIPT

🎧 **Track 10.2**

Hello everyone, and welcome to my webinar. My name is Kendra Phillips, and I'm going to give a short talk on the topic of medical tourism. Because this is a webinar, you can all hear me, but I cannot hear you. But you should see a small comment box in the upper right corner. Type questions for me, and I'll answer them at the end of my talk. So, let's get started. I'll begin now by answering the main question. What is medical tourism?

Medical tourism is the process of a person traveling to a foreign country to obtain medical treatment. It used to be that residents of less-developed countries traveled to more developed countries because they could not receive care in their home country. As you can see from this map, nowadays it's just as likely that people from more-developed countries travel to less-developed countries. So, which countries receive the most medical tourists? You can see here that the top five are Thailand, Hungary, India, Singapore, and Malaysia. But the countries traveled to often depend on the treatment you need. For example, Thailand attracts people who want cosmetic surgery. People go to Hungary for dental care, India for cardiac treatment, that is, matters to do with the heart, and Singapore for cancer treatment. For overall checkups and tests, Malaysia is popular.

The market for medical tourism is huge, at about 50 billion U.S. dollars a year. Fourteen million people go to other countries for treatment every year. They spend on average between $3,800 and $6,000 per visit. This may seem high but costs are generally much cheaper than in the patient's home country. And the market is growing fast; it is thought to be growing at a worldwide rate of between 15 and 25%. In certain countries the rate of growth each year is much higher than that—for example, 45–65% in Costa Rica and 65–90% in India. It's pretty clear that the medical tourism trend is going to be with us for a while.

So what's process for someone who is interested in medical tourism? First, the person contacts a medical tourism provider in the country they plan to go to. The tourism provider asks for a full medical report. Before making a recommendation, a doctor will give you information on the choice of doctor or hospital, how long the treatment is, and the cost. The provider then arranges the details and the patient travels to the country. The patient may need to pay for additional care if necessary. The doctor then says when the patient can fly home. This might be a good time to discuss the term "medical tourism" a bit more. As you can see it's not tourism exactly. It's just more of a marketing term. It's simply getting treatment in another country.

What are some advantages of medical tourism? The first is it's cheaper. The patient may not be able to afford the medical treatment in their own country. The amount the patient saves will depend on the country and the treatment type. According to the American Medical Association, a knee replacement costs between $41,000 and $59,000 in the U.S., but only $8,500 in India.

The second advantage of medical tourism allows patients to receive treatments that may not be available in their home country or that they would have to wait a long time to receive. In some countries, patients might have to wait, say, a year for a procedure, whereas in another country there may only be a short waiting list, or no waiting list at all.

Yet another plus is the quality of care. Many patients believe that the quality of care in countries that accept medical tourists is much lower. Not true. Most of these hospitals and clinics have excellent facilities that are often devoted to specific treatments. However, it is true that quality of care is not the same everywhere so patients should do their research before going.

There are drawbacks to medical tourism. One is the lack of follow-up care. A person may go overseas, receive treatment, then return home. Unfortunately, there is no or little follow up, which can be a serious problem if something goes wrong. The home country may then be responsible for the patient's care, which may cost more.

Another drawback is malpractice. Malpractice is what happens when a doctor's care is careless, wrong, or dangerous. In these cases, the patient understandably expects some sort of money to be paid back. Not all doctors have insurance for this, so a patient may not be able to do anything if they suffer from a doctor's malpractice abroad.

At this point let me take a few questions—oh, here's one already: *Can you tell me where someone might go for eye treatment?* Well, I suggest you do your own research, but I can say that Turkey is known for its excellent eye care.

OK, another question, this one is about gender. *Do you know what percentage of men are medical tourists?* Well, right now about 70% of medical tourists are women and 30% are men. Here I see someone asked about the effect on doctors who are too busy treating medical tourists, and have no time to treat patients at home. That's a great point, I think, and something people should definitely consider.

Final question. *Can you tell me if medical tourism is the same as wellness tourism?* Well, they both involve travel, but they are different. Wellness tourism is for those who are trying to prevent illness, perhaps by eating well or exercising differently. Medical tourists are looking for treatment.

I think that's it now, so thanks so much.

ANSWERS

1 Countries **2** The Top Five **3** Key Statistics
4 The Process **5** Benefits **6** Drawbacks

D Close listening

Listening to determine the speaker's attitude

Read through the *Listening to determine the speaker's attitude* box with the students. Focus on the example sentences, and the difference in connotation of *curious* and *nosy* (**Answer:** *nosy is negative, and implies behavior that is intrusive, and unasked for*). Model both sentences, giving more emphasis to *nosy*, as a speaker might when indicating their negative view.

Allow time for students to review the statements. Then play the audio. Stop after each excerpt, and ask students to discuss their answer with a partner. Go through the answers with the class. Then play the complete audio again, asking students to note down words and features of the excerpts which helped them to decide on the answer.

AUDIO SCRIPT

🎧 **Track 10.3**

1 This might be a good time to discuss the term "medical tourism" a bit more. As you can see it is not tourism exactly. It's just more of a marketing term. It's simply getting treatment in another country.

2 One is the lack of follow-up care. A person may go overseas, receive treatment, then return home. Unfortunately, there is no, or little follow up, which can be a serious problem if something goes wrong.

3 Malpractice is what happens when a doctor's care is careless, wrong, or dangerous. In these cases, the patient understandably expects some sort of money to be paid back.

4 Here I see someone asked about the effect on doctors who are too busy treating medical tourists, and have no time to treat patients at home. That's a great point, I think, and something people should definitely consider.

ANSWERS

1 F (He thinks it's more of a marketing term.) 2 T
3 F (He says that, understandably, the patient expects some sort of money to be paid back.) 4 T

E Critical thinking

Weighing up the pros and cons to reach a conclusion is an important part of critical thinking. In addition to simply weighing up the pros and cons, more complex issues may require some acknowledgement of opposing arguments, even though the person's overall view does not align with them. In this section, encourage students to come to an overall view of whether medical tourism is a good thing or not, but highlight that things are rarely "black and white" (i.e., *completely clear / 100% good or bad*).

Students discuss question 1 in small groups. Monitor and encourage discussion. Invite whole-class feedback, along with a show of hands to get the overall view of the class.

Students discuss the other questions. Share ideas as a whole class.

Extension activity

Compile a list of questions that the students would like to ask the webinar presenter. Then assign the task, in class or at home, for students to answer these questions. This may require a combination of research and opinion-giving, depending on the questions asked.

PRONUNCIATION

Pronunciation for listening
Linking the same consonant sounds

Allow time for students to read through the *Linking the same consonant sounds* box. Then, with books closed, asked students to explain the main idea and give you some examples of it. Highlight to students that the focus is on sounds, rather than letters, so, for example, the principle does not apply to *This is my topi**c c**hoice*.

1 Students identify the adjacent words which end, and then start, with the same consonant sound.

2 Students listen to the sentences and check their answers from Exercise 1.

AUDIO SCRIPT

🎧 Track 10.4

1 But let's see if it works.
2 I'll begin now by answering that question.
3 As you can see, it's not tourism exactly.
4 It's simply getting treatment in another country.
5 The amount the patient saves will depend on the country and the treatment type.
6 In these cases, the patient understandably expects some sort of money to be paid back

ANSWERS

1 But let's see if it works.
2 I'll begin now by answering that question.
3 As you can see, it is not tourism exactly.
4 It's simply getting treatment in another country.
5 The amount the patient saves will depend on the country and the treatment type.
6 In these cases, the patient understandably expects some sort of money to be paid back.

3 Students listen and complete the sentences. Allow time to check in pairs before playing the audio again.

AUDIO SCRIPT

🎧 Track 10.5

1 There are many things you can do to help prevent illness.
2 Be sure to ask your doctor if follow-up care is paid for by your insurance.
3 Don't make cosmetic surgery decisions without talking to several doctors.
4 Did you quit your job before you got new health insurance?
5 I was able to manage just enough time off work for my treatment.

ANSWERS

1 help prevent 2 if follow-up 3 make cosmetic
4 job before 5 manage just

VOCABULARY

Vocabulary development
Medical vocabulary

If the *Warm-up* exercise was used at the start of the unit, some of the words may have come up then. If this is the case, ask students to identify them.

1 Students work alone to match the words to the definitions. Allow time for students to compare their answers in pairs before going through the answers as a class. Model and drill the pronunciation with the class.

ANSWERS
1 e **2** d **3** a **4** b **5** c **6** h **7** i **8** f **9** g
10 j

2 Students work in pairs to complete the word web and add other words. Build up the word web on the board in whole-class feedback, adding the students' extra words.

ANSWERS
1 clinic, hospice, nursing home
2 cure, pill
3 home health aid, surgeon, therapist
4 disease, flu
Possible additional answers:
Places to receive care: hospital, health center
Things that help / make us feel good: medicine, treatments
People who give care: doctor, nurse
Things that harm / make us feel bad: a cold, a virus

3 Ask students to identify the target vocabulary words in the questions (**Answers:** *flu, clinic, surgeon, hospice*). Students then discuss the questions in pairs.

VOCABULARY

Academic words

1 In pairs, students discuss the words and sentences and choose the best definition. Go through the answers with the class.

ANSWERS
1 a **2** c **3** b **4** b **5** c **6** b **7** b

2 Students discuss the questions with a partner. When all the questions have been answered, put pairs together to open up the discussion. Ask groups to report back on points they disagreed on.

SPEAKING

Speaking model

Read through the aims of the *Speaking* section with students. Highlight that all work in the unit leads towards the successful completion of the final task. Ask students to underline the things they will learn in this section (**Answer:** *about using indirect questions, refuting arguments,* and *citations, contrastive,* and *emphatic stress*), and one thing they will do (**Answer:** *have a debate*).

A Analyze

1 and 2 Students read the excerpts from *Face-to-face vs. online doctors*. They follow the script in their books, underlining, and circling as instructed. After reading, the students compare answers with a partner's, and discuss the two questions.

ANSWERS
Saying the other side's argument is not true or accurate:
I don't think that's really true.
I'm afraid that's not accurate.
Two questions that are asked:
Do you know what percentage of people are happy to see online doctors?
Can you tell me what a second opinion is?
The questions are indirect in that they begin with *Do you know / Can you tell me* + a statement

B Discuss

Students discuss the questions with a partner. Monitor and encourage students to explain and justify their answers.

GRAMMAR

Indirect questions

With books closed, write on the board *Can you tell me what a second opinion is?* Remind students this is one of the questions from the model. Ask students if they remember the name of this grammar point from their review of the aims at the start of this section (**Answer:** *indirect questions*). Ask students what the direct question is (**Answer:** *What is a second opinion?*). Write this on the board, and ask students to analyze the differences between the two forms (**Answer:** *position of the verb*).

Students open their books and read through the *Indirect questions* box. Ask what happens when the question is a Yes / No question (**Answer:** *we use if*).

1 Students work alone to rewrite the questions. Allow time for students to check in pairs, and then go through the answers with the class.

> ANSWERS
> **1** Can you tell me what a good country for eye care is?
> **2** Do you know if my medical insurance covers hospice care?
> **3** (Do you know) when medical tourism first became popular?
> **4** (Do you remember) if your second opinion was the same as your first opinion?

2 Students work in pairs to find and correct the mistakes. Go through the answers with the class.

> ANSWERS
> **1** Do you know what the phone number of the hospital is?
> **2** Can you tell me if your doctor takes this type of insurance?
> **3** Do you have an idea how much the hospice charges each day?
> **4** Can you tell us when tomorrow's debate will begin?

3 Students work alone to write indirect questions in response to the arguments. They then compare their answers in pairs.

SPEAKING ▶

Speaking skill
Refuting an argument

Warm-up

Say the following (and write on the board if necessary): *Students should do three hours of homework every day.* Say this is what you believe, but invite students to argue against you (keep individual arguments against this short, and invite a few students to respond). Listen to the different arguments, using facial expressions to show what you think of them. Then as students continue to refute your argument, write up *You said that … but …,* and indicate that students should incorporate this into their refutation. Then add *That's not true, because … ,* and *That may be true, but in fact …* again indicating that students should use these phrases. Invite some students who have already spoken to reformulate their arguments using these phrases. Show greater acceptance of the argument after it has been reformulated. Then ask students to explain what the phrases do (**Possible answer:** *state the argument, and provide support for the counter argument*).

Students read through the information in the *Refuting an argument* box. Check the meaning of words as necessary (e.g., *accurate, claim*—highlight that the use of this suggests that the person does not believe the "claim").

1 Students work in pairs to match the arguments to the best way to refute them.

> ANSWERS
> **1** b **2** d **3** e **4** c **5** a

2 Students listen and check their answers.

AUDIO SCRIPT

🎧 **Track 10.6**

1 Hospice care can be expensive.

There's some truth to that, but many patients feel more comfortable there than a hospital.

2 You are more likely to get a cold when it's cold outside.

That's not true because there is no evidence of a link with temperature.

3 Seeing doctors face-to-face is not very convenient.

There's some truth to your argument, but I think it's safer because they can examine you up close, and not via video.

4 Drinking a lot of liquids can help you get over a cold.

That may be true, but in fact the best way is simply to rest.

5 Online doctors are completely ineffective for illnesses that aren't visible, like headaches.

I'm afraid that's not accurate because I know many illnesses can be detected from a distance.

3 Read through the task with students. Then students take turns to state and refute arguments. Monitor and make a note of successful and less successful use of the target phrases. Use these notes in whole-class feedback, encouraging students to identify the successful language use, and reformulate the less effective parts.

PRONUNCIATION ▶

Pronunciation for speaking
Citation, contrastive, and emphatic stress

Warm-up

With books closed, on the board write the following: *"What did you say?" "I said nurse." / I went to the doctor on Tuesday, not Thursday. / That is cheap, but medical tourism is much cheaper.* Model the sentences for the students, and ask them to identify the most stressed word in each (**Answers:** *nurse, Tuesday,* and *much*). Ask students to suggest why those particular words are stressed. Listen to the answers, and then ask students to open their books and read through the *Citation, contrastive, and emphatic stress* box. Then ask students to explain again in their own words.

1   Students listen to the sentences and underline the stressed word. They compare their answers in pairs, and also discuss what type of stress it was (i.e., *citation*, *contrastive*, or *emphatic*).

AUDIO SCRIPT

🎧 Track 10.7

1   We believe that an online doctor can tell what is wrong with a patient.
2   Yes, I mean, no.
3   That may be true, but it's a big concern.
4   What do you mean, no?
5   In that case, you are spending more money.

ANSWERS
1 can—emphatic   **2** no—contrastive   **3** big—emphatic
4 no—citation   **5** more—contrastive

---

2   Students review the conversation with a partner and underline the possible stressed words. They also identify the type of stress used. They then listen and check.

AUDIO SCRIPT

🎧 Track 10.8

A: These instructions on my prescription are really hard to read. What does this say?
B: It says p.m. That means evening.
A: Ah, so I take the medicine in the evening.
B: Well, not only in the evening. You need to take it in the morning, too.
A: So I take a pill twice a day.
B: No, you take two pills twice a day.
A: OK, thanks. I don't think I need a medical doctor. I need an eye doctor!

ANSWERS
A: really (emphatic), **B:** p.m. (citation), evening (emphatic),
B: only (contrastive), **A:** twice (emphatic), **B:** two
(contrastive), **B:** medical (contrastive), eye (contrastive)

---

3   Students practice the conversation in pairs. Monitor the discussions, helping students with their use of citation, contrastive, and emphatic stress where necessary.

SPEAKING ▶

Speaking task

Warm-up

Have a unit test on the content of this unit. Put students into teams, and give them a set amount of time to review the unit (e.g., 20 minutes). Tell them what the test will focus on (e.g., *information from the listenings / grammar / vocabulary / a combination*). As students review the unit, prepare questions. Students then answer the questions in a quiz format. Award one point for each correct answer.

Brainstorm and plan

1   Put the students into small groups. Read through the statement, and highlight that at this stage, they are thinking about both sides of the issue.

2   Students brainstorm reasons to support both sides of the argument. Highlight the ideas in the book to support this discussion. Students note their reasons in a table. Monitor and assist as necessary, encouraging students to think of a whole range of reasons.

Each group splits into two sides. Each side follows the planning stages to prepare for the debate. Again, monitor and assist, particularly focusing the students' attention on developing arguments to refute the other side's points.

Speak and share

Students have the debate. If appropriate, and equipment is available, record the debate for students to review later.

As students have their debates, monitor and note successful and less successful language use in the key areas of the unit.

Students then form new groups. They share the key points of the debate. They also identify which side they considered to be the stronger, and why.

Have a feedback session on language use. Share the examples you noted, and highlight effective language use. For less successful language use, encourage peer correction, and help the students to reformulate the language.

Reflect

Allow time for students to reflect alone on the questions. They then share their reflections with their original debate group. If the debate was recorded earlier, this would be a good time to review it.

REVIEW

Wordlist

Students work in pairs or small groups to work through the *Wordlist*, checking that they all remember what each word or phrase means, how to pronounce it, and how it was used in the unit. Go through the list carefully with the class.

Academic words review

Students work through the sentences. Ask students to check their answers in pairs, and then check as a class.

> ANSWERS
> **1** procedure   **2** guarantee   **3** vision   **4** medical
> **5** residents

Unit review

Students work through the list alone to decide what they can and can't do. They discuss their answers in pairs, including what they remember from the unit about each point. Finally, open up the discussion to include the whole class. Pay particular attention to any boxes that the students didn't check. Explore with them ways of overcoming any remaining problems.

Extra research task

As a take-home activity, ask students to research a medical advancement with technology. This could be something happening now, or something that will happen in the future. Students present information on the advancement in the next lesson. One of these could be chosen to form the basis of another group debate.

VIDEO SCRIPTS

Unit 1: Society

NARRATOR: The Duke and Duchess of Cambridge have connections with many charities throughout the U.K., and around the world.

Child Bereavement U.K. is just one of hundreds of thousands of charities in the U.K. alone. The young royals William and Kate like to "do their bit for society" by supporting various charities like this one.

NARRATOR: The Duchess works with charities that help young families with children.

NARRATOR: She goes to visit the centers to meet young mothers and find out how the charity helps them. Today, she is at the Anna Freud National Centre for Children and Families. She is learning about how the charity helps children under five years old. She also talks to the mothers to find out about their lives and their children.

NARRATOR: Like Kate, William also visits the charities that he supports to meet families, staff, and volunteers—people who work with the charity for free. Volunteers give help to those people who need it but help isn't just food, clothes, or money—there are many other ways you can support charities by offering advice and your time as a volunteer, like William and Kate are doing in this center.

NARRATOR: Today, they are both visiting the Child Bereavement U.K. charity because it is the center's one-year anniversary of its opening.

NARRATOR: A cake has been made to celebrate the success of the charity, and the Royals have been asked to cut the cake to start the celebrations.

Unit 2: Food

NARRATOR: Students at the National University of Singapore are doing some exciting new research into environmentally friendly plastic that provides a healthier way to keep food. Tan Yi Min is one of the students testing this new type of plastic to store bread, and explains why it is better for our health and why we should start using it.

TAN YI MIN: Most of the normal plastic that we use to wrap food contains chemicals. These can go into the food and then into our bodies when we eat the food. The chemicals can cause health issues that affect our brains, so that's one of the possible impacts.

NARRATOR: Tan makes this new type of plastic from natural products such as crabs, shrimps, and grapefruits. She takes some chitosan powder, which is made from crab shells and shells of other sea animals, and pours it into a bottle.

Tan adds more ingredients into the bottle and mixes them together. She pours the liquid into a glass dish. When the liquid is dry, it makes a type of plastic.

Tan wraps two pieces of bread in two types of plastic to see how well each piece of bread stays fresh. After 20 days, she looks at both pieces of bread again. You can see that the bread on the left, in the normal polyethylene plastic has lots of green mold. The bread on the right, wrapped in the new chitosan-based packaging, has no mold.

Tan and her colleague test the bread. The bread stored in the new type of plastic was kept fresher for longer: A great result!

Unit 3: Business

NARRATOR: This is a busy street in New York City, and this is Erica. She is looking for a quiet office space where she can take a break in between meetings in the city. She's using a new app on her phone, called Breather, to find a building that rents offices by the hour. The app uses a map and shows you photos of the offices that are available. The app is called Breather because "having a breather," means taking a break.

Now that she's found the building, Erica chooses an office space and buys an hour.

PACKY MCCORMICK: Breather is a network of beautiful private spaces available in major cities, right now in Montreal and New York, that you can find, reserve, and access via our mobile app.

NARRATOR: Now that she has bought an hour of office space, the app sends her a passcode that she can use to open the door.

The office looks just like the photo on the app, but Erica doesn't just use the office space to work. She sits down to take a breather from traveling all over the busy New York streets from meeting to meeting.

ERICA GENEREUX SMITH: I'm always all over the city every day. I have different things to do in different parts of town, different appointments—and I can't always go home in between, and I don't necessarily want to go to a coffee shop or just hang out. So, I would definitely use it, sort of, you know, if I had an awkward amount of time.

NARRATOR: Breather's office space is convenient because she doesn't always want to spend hours and hours in coffee shops.

The New York City manager of Breather, Packy McCormick, also says that people don't always rent their offices to work.

PACKY MCCORMICK: So we love people having meetings, we love people coming to take a nap, we love people coming to do their homework, all of that you can do. Use your imagination for what you can do.

NARRATOR: Breather has some rules for what people can and can't do in the office spaces. It wouldn't be fair if people used the room for band rehearsal if their neighbors were trying to work or rest next door. To me, it looks like a great place to work.

Unit 4: Trends

NARRATOR: More and more motor manufacturers are making autonomous vehicles in the form of driverless cars. These companies believe that driverless cars will be safer. However, this does not mean that driverless cars will never crash.

Octo USA is a company that studies information to discover the cause of crashes. They help companies analyze statistics from car accidents to see who or what is to blame.

JONATHAN HEWETT: Autonomous vehicles do crash, and, you know, this is something that will continue to happen because, at the moment, we don't have autonomous pedestrians or autonomous cyclists.

NARRATOR: Mr. Hewett suggests problems are caused by driverless cars driving in normal traffic. Here we can see possible problems such as cyclists wearing headphones but no safety equipment, as well as buses and pedestrians.

Drivers are normally responsible for a crash, but if driverless cars crash, the manufacturer might be responsible and may need to pay lots of money if someone sues them.

JONATHAN HEWETT: The roads are going to be a difficult and complicated space, and in that complicated space, the data and the analytics to know precisely who is doing what at any given time is immutable, it's something that we have to know. Motor manufacturers need to know whether it's their hardware or software at fault or whether it's the driver, and what the dynamic is when other third parties are involved.

NARRATOR: Manufacturers are spending lots of money to analyze data to discover why a driverless car crashes and see who or what is to blame. The type of data that they receive records the angle, the speed, and where the crash happened. Perhaps this information will help prevent crashes in the future and make driverless cars safer.

Unit 5: Success

NARRATOR: There's a new type of coding school in the U.S. growing in popularity, and we are going to hear why the school is such a success.

Two years ago, Walter Latimer was a student at Wyncode Academy. After studying art for a couple of years and not finding employment, he decided he needed further skills to help him find a job. Walter registered for an intensive, ten-week computer coding course at Wyncode. He graduated successfully, and is now a Product Manager at an education company in Silicon Valley.

Walter says that the ten-week course in this type of school is good for those students who can't or don't want to go to university to learn coding. Instead, success is based on merit, the effort you make, and how hard you study.

WALTER LATIMER: There's a really great opportunity there for people who maybe don't have that traditional schooling, or maybe didn't, you know, get into the top schools, but still have it in them to really succeed because it's really more merit based at this point.

NARRATOR: To get a computer programming job you normally need to go to university to get a three-year degree in computer science. However, Walter says technology moves so fast that it is a good idea to go to a coding school to learn the skills you need instead of traditional education.

WALTER LATIMER: Technology has created a whole new set of rules and traditional education can't really keep up with those, and so now we're seeing more people needing to just kind of get trained, like, as needed.

NARRATOR: So an intensive course in a coding school like this helps you learn the skills and be successful in getting the employment that you want, working with computers. The Managing Director explains why the academy has become a success story, and what she asks employers.

JOHANNA MIKKOLA: We look for real-time feedback from all of our hiring partners, and we ask those 100 partners what technology they need these individuals to know and learn because, for us, outcomes are so important. So if we're not teaching what our hiring partners and employers need, you know, it's not going to work out in the end.

Unit 6: Pressure

NARRATOR: Tokyo, Japan. Minoru Kagata has just finished a day's work and is going to an evening class for his hobby. Minoru is one of the 15 million people in Japan whose hobby is flower arranging. After work, he goes to a florist to buy flowers which he will use in the class.

Minoru is 62 years old and married with no children. He explains why he first started going to flower arranging classes 20 years ago.

MINORU KAGATA: When I was 42, I hurt my back skiing and I stayed in bed for a whole week. After that, I decided to do something creative instead of a sport.

NARRATOR: In this school, you can see that flower arranging is more popular with men than women. Flowers are chosen for their color, shape, and size. Students decide where to put the flowers in a vase and then cut the flowers and branches to the correct size.

So why do people go to the flower arranging class? Koji is 44 years old and works as a language teacher. Working with flowers adds something different to his life and relaxes his busy mind after a stressful day at work. He says that he does it to connect to the world.

It might seem surprising that men in Tokyo are taking part in flower arranging as a hobby. However, it was usually men who did flower arranging when it started in Japan 500 years ago. In today's pressurized world, working with flowers is a change of direction and speed for businessmen with stressful jobs. Gaho Isono, Master Instructor at a flower arrangement school, agrees.

GAHO ISONO: I think that a lot of people are looking for alternative ways to calm down after work. There is no reason why men can't do flower arranging, and we see an increasing number of men taking flower arrangement classes like this.

NARRATOR: The whole process is very creative and relaxing, and students feel proud of their work. Do you think you could make beautiful and creative pieces of art using flowers, like these?

Unit 7: Fear

NARRATOR: This is the skyline over Los Angeles, California. The photo was taken from a slide that is on the outside of a skyscraper.

The slide is made of very strong glass and is attached to one of the tallest buildings in Los Angeles. You slide for 45 feet or 14 meters. At the end, you land on the 69th floor.

The sky slide is 1,000 feet, or 300 meters above the streets of Los Angeles. It's not a place to be if you have vertigo or acrophobia, a fear of heights. The glass is only one and a quarter inches or 3.2 cm thick, but the glass is normally used in places where they have hurricanes and earthquakes.

JOHN GAMBOA: Safety was our top priority when we were developing this slide. You know, it's ready to withstand hurricane-level winds. The glass actually is similar to the glass they use in Florida to prevent against damage from destructive hurricane winds. The steel is aerospace-engineered steel in some components, so it's very technologically sound. The slide itself can withstand an eight on the Richter scale for an earthquake.

NARRATOR: So, what is the experience like? This woman explains that you go faster than you expect.

REBECCA FITZGERALD: You go around in a curve pushed up against the glass. It's like you see the whole world below you. But it's not really that scary.

NARRATOR: So, one person thinks it is not scary, but what do other people think? This woman is afraid of heights and wanted to face her fear.

KERI FREEMAN: I thought it was nerve-wracking, and exciting and, like, daring … and I just had to do it because I'm so afraid of heights and I just wanted to break that fear.

NARRATOR: Los Angeles is not well-known for its tall buildings.

ANTONIO PACHECO: I think that this is weird for L.A. because we don't really do, like, skydecks or, you know, viewing platforms because we don't have that many tall buildings, so it's exciting to have this available to people as a place to come up and kind of see and enjoy the city. I think it's cool.

NARRATOR: Would you dare to go down this slide to see these amazing views?

Unit 8: Stories

NARRATOR: This wheel is the Singapore Flyer. It measures 165 meters in height, about the height of a 42-storey building. If you look very carefully, you will see someone in orange.

That person is Alain Robert, but some people call him "The French Spiderman." Like Spiderman, Alain climbs up extremely tall buildings, normally using just his bare hands and no safety equipment.

Alain doesn't usually wear safety gear, but today he is at the Singapore Mettle Games, an action sports event.

Alain explains that nowadays he has to deal with the authorities regularly, and as a result, he has a lawyer to help him.

However, even with safety gear, climbing up tall structures makes everyday activities like drinking water seem difficult. Luckily, he doesn't suffer from vertigo.

Alain looks around him to admire the amazing Singapore skyline, including the incredible Singapore Opera House.

Today he is more nervous about the weather than vertigo. The rain makes the surface slippery when wet. He looks around to check the weather.

He tells reporters at a conference how he felt.

ALAIN ROBERT: No, actually today I was having to think about the weather. You know, the weather was a bit threatening.

NARRATOR: Alain has climbed more than 80 buildings around the world, including what was Chicago's Sears Tower, Taiwan's tallest tower, the Taipei 101, and of course, the Eiffel Tower in his home country, France. Climbing today, however, Alain said he was not taking any risks.

ALAIN ROBERT: By climbing the Singapore Flyer I was using some safety from bottom to top to bottom, and then I was not really taking any risk.

NARRATOR: Luckily, he made it safe and sound at the top of the Singapore Flyer.

Unit 9: Environment

NARRATOR: What color are British phone boxes? Red? Not always. This public phone box in London has turned green. But, green is not just the color of the box, it also stands for its environmental status. This green phone box is also a charging station for mobile devices. But why does that make it environmentally friendly? This phone box has a solar panel on its roof to turn solar power into electricity.

Two graduates from the London School of Economics came up with the idea and received competition money to build a prototype model for future solar-powered phone boxes.

Kirsty is one of the inventors. What does she think about environmental problems in London and the Solarbox?

KIRSTY KENNEY: London is still a city very much built for cars and I think, you know, on the everyday level, we're not actually that green. And it's not the fault of the public, the infrastructure isn't there yet. Perhaps that will inspire people to think a little bit and think about what they might be able to do or what they might like to do.

NARRATOR: Harold is the other co-inventor. He explains why we should use Solarbox.

HAROLD CRASTON: Phones are getting more powerful and apps are getting more complex. Phones are actually, in the last few years, getting larger again, but the batteries, they're not .... So, until that happens, there will be a reason to use Solarbox and celebrate solar power.

NARRATOR: So, phones and apps are using up more battery power and a Solarbox will help you when your phone runs out of power. The public is definitely interested in the Solarbox, but is it to charge their phones … or just take photos of it with their phones? Time will tell when more Solarboxes pop up in the future.

Unit 10: Medicine

NARRATOR: The parks of New York City. What on earth is the connection between the dirt that you find in parks and research into modern medicine? Two scientists from a university lab at Rockefeller University think they have the answer. Dr. Sean Brady and Zach Charlop-Powers are digging up earth from parks in New York to study the bacteria that's found in that dirt, then they take the dirt to their laboratory to see if the genes from the dirt's bacteria contain molecules that can be used in antibiotics and cancer treatments.

Dr. Brady explains how molecules are normally found. Usually you would culture or grow bacteria in a laboratory to find molecules. Here are some Petri dishes that show signs of activity.

DR. SEAN BRADY: The traditional approach for finding molecules that would be therapies from bacteria is that you culture bacteria.

NARRATOR: The advantage, however, to finding bacteria and molecules in dirt is that you can find dirt near the laboratory, instead of traveling to other environments.

DR. SEAN BRADY: Maybe we don't have to go to these rare environments or environments that are endangered to go find some of these molecules.

ZACH CHARLOP-POWERS: Many of the molecules that we've used in the clinic have historically been isolated from organisms that have their origin all over the world.

NARRATOR: Did you know that half of all medicines used today were once found in bacteria, animals, or plants from planet Earth? Earth contains around five million trillion trillion types of bacteria, according to an estimate in 1998, by scientists at the University of Georgia.

Next time you take your medicine, you might just remember where it came from.

ANSWER KEY

UNIT 1

SOCIETY

Discussion point
Students' own answers

Video

Before you watch
1 F (They also give food, clothes, advice, and time.)
2 T
3 T
4 F (Prince William also works with charities.)

While you watch
1 Charities that help young families with children.
2 Volunteers give help to people who need it.
3 It's the center's one-year anniversary of opening.
4 two

After you watch
Students' own answers

Listening 1

A Vocabulary preview
1
1 c   2 c   3 a   4 a   5 c   6 a   7 b   8 b
2
1 fortunate
2 institution
3 donate
4 community service
5 duty
6 consider
7 concept
8 recommendations

B Before you listen
Students' own answers

C Global listening
✓ Community service includes volunteering time, and service to help others.
✓ Volunteers work in different types of public institutions.
✓ Caring about others has nothing to do with the person helping, it's about the people receiving the help.

D Close listening
1
Community service – volunteering
Community institutions – schools, hospitals
Work at hospitals – visit patients, help doctors and nurses, read to the blind, work with people with disabilities
Types of manual work – planting trees, building a house
2
1 For example
2 For instance
3 like
4 such as

E Critical thinking
Students' own answers

Study skills
Students' own answers

Listening 2

A Vocabulary preview
1
1 g   2 d   3 a   4 b   5 c   6 e   7 f   8 h

2
1 experiment
2 cause
3 expensive
4 original
5 provide
6 colleague
7 opposite
8 charity

B Before you listen
2
1 Ask a question about the experiment
2 Describe the experiment
3 Describe the results
4 Answer the question about the experiment

C Global listening
1 charity, happiness
2 college students
3 help others
4 happier
5 small, big
6 team

D Close listening
1 and 2
Possible answers
Question professor wants to answer
    Can money buy happiness?
Describe experiment
    College students in Canada
    Each given an envelope of money
    Half told to spend it on themselves
    Half told to spend it on others
    Also conducted in Uganda
    Also conducted on sales teams at a company
Describe results
    Those that spent money on others were happier.
    It didn't matter how much money it was.
    It didn't matter what the money was spent on—big things, or small things.
Answer the question
    Money can buy happiness … when you spend it on others.

E Critical thinking
Students' own answers

Pronunciation for listening
1
1 every /'evri/
2 comparable /'kɒmp(ə)rəb(ə)l/
3 generally /'dʒenrəli/
4 different /'dɪfrənt/
5 favorite /'feɪvrɪt/
6 reasonable /'riznəbl/
7 suppose /spoʊz/
8 miserable /'mɪzrəbəl/

Vocabulary development
1
1 do
2 give
3 make
4 answer
5 manage
6 order
7 take
8 pay
2
Students' own answers

Academic words
1
1 h   2 g   3 b   4 a   5 f   6 e   7 d   8 c
2
Students' own answers

Speaking model
A Analyze
1 a   2 c   3 b

B Discuss

1 Most of the money actually goes to people.
2 I think, In addition, it also

Grammar

1
Possible answers
1 You can volunteer at the hospital because they need people to visit patients. Also, they need people to help the nurses.
2 Jana worked for 16 hours without a break and she needs to sleep. Plus, she doesn't want to get sick.
3 Peter might do work experience at the hospital because he wants to go to medical school. Furthermore, he wants to help sick people.
4 Lily should become president of the volunteer group because she volunteers the most hours. What's more, she knows a lot of charities.
5 Kenichi donated all his clothes to the less fortunate. In addition, he donated some money to the food bank in his local community.

2 and 3
Students' own answers

Speaking skill

1
1 may be because
2 due to, resulting in
3 One consequence of
4 may be due to

2
Possible answers
Small charities might give more money to people they help because:
they have less overhead costs.
they don't need to pay as many employees.
they have less to pay on building rent, bills, and administration because there are fewer employees.
They might not give as much money to people they help because:
they rely on the money more to pay staff wages.
they get less financial support than large charities, so more donation money is needed to help run, and support the charity.

Pronunciation for speaking

1
1 7   2 8   3 10   4 8   5 7   6 8

2
1 I went to the market today to buy apples.
2 Daniel wrote an essay about volunteering in his home country.
3 Julie and Nadia are in the same class.
4 My teacher said that I have to study for my test.

Speaking task
Students' own answers

Review

Academic words review
1 revision
2 principal
3 normal
4 benefit
5 intermediate

FOOD

Discussion point
Students' own answers

Video

Before you watch

1
1 Food is wasted when it is not eaten; too much food is produced; it goes off / out of date.
2 *Possible answers*: Some food which is out of date is still OK to eat, stores put a date that is "best eaten before," but doesn't mean it's bad to eat it; it might make you sick if you eat food that has gone bad / gone off.

3 Moldy: fruit, bread (if stored in plastic), cheese; Stale (if left in the open air): cookies, bread, cake
4 If it's out of date; if food is left out of a fridge / stored badly; oxygen reaches the food and makes it moldy / stale.
5 *Students' own answers*

2 and 3
Students' own answers

While you watch
plastic, bread, crab shells, bottles, mold
Possible answer: These things are all part of an experiment in the video which researches environmentally friendly plastic.

After you watch
1 Normal *polyethylene* plastic makes bread go moldy after a few days; an environmental impact is also plastic pollution. (According to Harvard University's Wyss Institute, humans produce 300 million tons of plastic per year … the remaining 97% is dumped in landfills, and oceans, harming the food chain, and the environment.)
2 It doesn't contain bad chemicals for your body (other possible answer: it is biodegradable, and better for the environment).
3 *Students' own answers*

Listening 1

A Vocabulary preview

1
1 g   2 d   3 a   4 e   5 c   6 h   7 f   8 b

2
1 challenge
2 hunger
3 feed
4 waste
5 agriculture
6 billion
7 profit
8 solution

B Before you listen
Students' own answers

C Global listening
1 In other words,
2 It's important to note that
3 In general,
4 Overall,

D Close listening

1
1 Sofia
2 Amira
3 Julia

2
1 B   2 C   3 B   4 A   5 A

E Critical thinking
Students' own answers

Study skills
Students' own answers

Listening 2

A Vocabulary preview

1
1 a   2 a   3 a   4 a   5 b   6 b   7 a   8 b

2
Students' own answers

B Before you listen
Students' own answers

C Global listening

1
Students' own answers

2
1 Because they are "good" for the brain.
2 dark chocolate, fish, coffee, cereal, milk, blueberries
3 They can improve how much you learn, your mental health, and your physical health.

D Close listening

1

1 c   2 a   3 b

2

1 similar   5 dark
2 memory   6 breakfast
3 short   7 cannot
4 chocolate

E Critical thinking
Students' own answers

Pronunciation for listening

1

1 out   5 up
2 to   6 out
3 out   7 about
4 on

2

1 moved on from /muvd ɑn frɑm/
2 take over /teɪk ˈoʊvər/
3 runs away from /rʌnz əˈweɪ frɑm/
4 get ahead of /gɛt əˈhɛd əv/

Vocabulary development

1

1 e   2 f   3 d   4 c   5 b   6 a

2

1 get up   4 point out
2 give up   5 throw out
3 turn into   6 find out

3
Students' own answers

Academic words

1

1 d   2 c   3 e   4 a   5 h   6 f   7 g   8 b

2
Students' own answers

Speaking model

A Analyze

1 there are over 100,000 inhabitants
2 the things they don't want
3 providing more waste bins
4 to clean up the streets

B Discuss
Students' own answers

Grammar

1 and 2

1 The last time we saw each other was <u>when we were in Mrs. Kingston's class.</u>
2 The store <u>where I usually buy my stationery</u> is closed.
3 The man, <u>whose job it is to fix the computers,</u> hasn't finished.
4 The students, <u>whose grades were low,</u> had to retake the test.
5 Two thousand sixteen was <u>when I graduated school.</u>
6 I remember the day <u>when I got my exam grades.</u> I was very nervous. [Relative pronoun can be removed.]

3

1 The woman, whose job it is to order books, is a library assistant.
2 Eduardo, whose exam is tomorrow, is studying.
3 Last week, when we did the experiment, it failed.
4 Spain, where it can get very hot in the summer, is a popular tourist destination.

Speaking skill

1

1 One idea is donating more food to charities.
2 I'd recommend avoiding eating too much food in the evening.
3 How about buying imperfect fruit at the market?
4 It might be a good idea to save food from ending up in the landfills.
5 I suggest using leftover food for compost or to feed farm animals.
6 You should buy food from the "ugly" section of the market.

2, 3, and 4
Students' own answers

Pronunciation for speaking

1

1 clue   5 free from
2 braise   6 green glasses
3 flame   7 clean room
4 fly   8 brew tea

2, 3, and 4
Students' own answers

Speaking task
Students' own answers

Review

Academic words review

1 debate   4 statistics
2 labels   5 normal
3 physical

UNIT 3
BUSINESS

Discussion point
Students' own answers

Video

Before you watch
Students' own answers

While you watch

1 and 2

1 c   2 a   3 e   4 b   5 d

After you watch
Students' own answers

Listening 1

A Vocabulary preview

1

1 d   2 a   3 c   4 b   5 g   6 e   7 h   8 f

2

1 seem   5 set up
2 cubicle   6 result
3 I guess   7 height
4 emerge   8 effect

B Before you listen
Students' own answers

C Global listening

1 open-plan spaces
2 closed offices
3 cubicles
4 desks
5 shared spaces
6 combination of office space

D Close listening

1

1 O   2 C   3 O   4 O   5 C

2

1 people	6 less
2 less	7 more
3 more	8 more
4 less	9 together
5 workers	

E Critical thinking
Students' own answers

Study skills
Students' own answers

Listening 2

A Vocabulary preview
1
1 a   2 e   3 f   4 d   5 b   6 c   7 h   8 g

2

1 achievement	5 part-time
2 introduce	6 friendships
3 create	7 sales
4 efficient	8 allow

3
Students' own answers

B Before you listen
Students' own answers

C Global listening
1 b   2 c   3 a   4 c   5 c

D Close listening
1

1 live	3 each
2 its	4 matter

2
1 1971
2 employees
3 customers
4 communication
5 customer service
6 good benefits
7 Achievement

E Critical thinking
Students' own answers

Pronunciation for listening
1

1 rise	3 fall
2 fall	4 rise

2 and 3
Students' own answers

Vocabulary development
1
1 a   2 c   3 b   4 d   5 h   6 g   7 f   8 e

2

1 suggestion	4 unemployment
2 realistic	5 triple
3 double	6 realistic

Academic words
1
1 b   2 b   3 b   4 a   5 b   6 b   7 a   8 a

2

1 indicate	5 revision
2 specify	6 academic
3 evolving	7 policy
4 definite	8 paragraph

Speaking model
1

1 sales	3 communication
2 worse	4 less

2
One suggestion is that … They should also …

B Discuss
Students' own answers

Grammar
1
Possible answers
1 shouldn't
2 could / may / might
3 might / may
4 should
5 could / may / might
6 should
7 should / may / might
8 could / might

2

1 should	4 want
2 sell	5 could
3 have	6 shouldn't

Speaking skill
1
1 interrupting
2 saying you are not finished
3 encouraging others to speak

2 and 3
Students' own answers

Pronunciation for speaking
1 and 2
Possible answers

My <u>presentation</u> <u>today</u> | is about how <u>Julio</u> and <u>Marcus</u> | can im<u>prove</u> things at <u>work</u> | so that they can <u>start</u> making more <u>money</u> | for the <u>business</u>.
<u>Julio</u> has said | that the <u>reason</u> <u>why</u> | he is <u>having</u> <u>problems</u> at <u>work</u> | is be<u>cause</u> he has a <u>family</u>. | A <u>lot</u> of people have <u>babies</u> and <u>families</u> | and they <u>still</u> <u>have</u> to <u>work</u>.
<u>People</u> <u>need</u> | to be <u>able</u> to <u>balance</u> | their <u>work</u> <u>lives</u> | with their <u>family</u> <u>lives</u>. | <u>Julio</u> and <u>Marcus</u> need to es<u>tablish</u> ways | to <u>overcome</u> this. | <u>One</u> suggestion is that | they have a <u>split</u> <u>schedule</u>. | In <u>other</u> words, | <u>Marcus</u> could work <u>earlier</u> in the <u>morning</u> | because <u>Julio</u> needs to come in <u>later</u>. | Then, | <u>Julio</u> could work <u>later</u> in the <u>evening</u>.
They would then work the <u>same</u> <u>number</u> of <u>hours</u> | and Marcus would <u>not</u> be doing <u>double</u> the <u>work</u>. | <u>Julio</u> has to <u>take</u> the <u>late</u> <u>shift</u> | so that he can <u>sleep</u> <u>later</u> in the <u>morning</u>. | I <u>think</u>, | if <u>they</u> do <u>this</u>, | they will <u>both</u> do <u>the</u> same <u>amount</u> of <u>work</u>. | They should <u>also</u> <u>specify</u> a <u>time</u> to <u>meet</u> | in the <u>middle</u> of <u>each</u> <u>day</u> | so that they can <u>make</u> <u>sure</u> they are getting <u>everything</u> <u>done</u>.
In <u>conclusion</u>, | <u>communicating</u> and <u>changing</u> the <u>schedule</u> | would be an <u>easy</u> <u>way</u> to make <u>both</u> of them <u>happy</u>, | and help in<u>crease</u> company <u>profits</u>. | <u>Profits</u> could be <u>checked</u> on a <u>bi</u>-annual <u>basis</u> | to make <u>sure</u> this new <u>policy</u> works.

Speaking task
Students' own answers

Review
Academic words review

1 policy	4 academic
2 paragraph	5 indicate
3 strategy	

UNIT 4
TRENDS

Discussion point
Students' own answers

Video
Before you watch
1 c 2 a 3 e 4 b 5 d

While you watch
1 safer
2 do crash sometimes
3 normal traffic
4 might be
5 who or what is to blame

After you watch
Students' own answers

Listening 1
A Vocabulary preview
1
1 h 2 c 3 d 4 a 5 b 6 g 7 f 8 e
2
1 passengers
2 anti-lock brakes
3 invented
4 wheels
5 seat belts
6 regulations
7 airbag
8 rear
3
Students' own answers

B Before you listen
Students' own answers

C Global listening
1 B D E   2 G I

D Close listening
1
1958 – Seat belts introduced
1966 – Anti-lock brakes introduced
1981 – Airbags introduced
1994 – First crash tests
1966 – First car to get a five-star rating
2
1 a 2 b 3 b 4 c

E Critical thinking
Students' own answers

Study skills
Students' own answers

Listening 2
A Vocabulary preview
1
1 h 2 f 3 e 4 g 5 a 6 b 7 d 8 c
2
1 T 2 F 3 F 4 T 5 T 6 F 7 T 8 F

B Before you listen
1
Students' own answers
2
blue: central business district
purple: inner city
green: inner suburbs
yellow: outer suburbs

C Global listening
1 b 3 a
2 b

D Close listening
1
Possible answers
Ancient times = Babylon and China saw considerable urban sprawl
Nearly 3,000 years ago = early Roman population started to spread outward
17th and 18th centuries = London experienced urban sprawl
Early 1900s = urban sprawl began in the U.S.
1918 = immigration resulted in greater urban growth
1940s and 1950s = government policies contributed to urban sprawl
1970s = urban sprawl became a social phenomenon
Present day = inner city populations are at all-time lows
2
1 a 2 b 3 a

E Critical thinking
Students' own answers

Pronunciation for listening
1
1 the 1960s
2 1918
3 the 1970s
2
Students' own answers

Vocabulary development
1
boring – uninteresting – exciting
crowded – busy – quiet
modern – new – ancient
safe – secure – dangerous
dirty – filthy – clean
expensive – valuable – cheap
famous – well-known – unknown
2
2 modern   5 cheap

Academic words
1
1 h 2 e 3 c 4 f 5 b 6 g 7 a 8 d
2
Students' own answers

Speaking model
A Analyze
1 history   2 ask questions
B Discuss
Students' own answers

Grammar
1
1 researched
2 lived
3 was, ended
4 happened
2
1 so that
2 because
3 since
4 in order to

Speaking skill
Students' own answers

Pronunciation for speaking
1 and 2
1 The process of buying a car isn't usually <u>quick</u> and <u>easy</u>.
2 There are <u>positives</u> and <u>negatives</u> to owning a car; it's not all good.
3 I like <u>peace</u> and <u>quiet</u>, so electric cars are my favorite.
4 Pinar would not tell us where she is going to college. We will have to <u>wait</u> and <u>see</u>.
5 She's very talented; she gets top grades in <u>arts</u> and <u>sciences</u>.

Speaking task
Students' own answers

Review
Academic words review
1 react
2 specifically
3 Furthermore
4 eventually
5 considerable

UNIT 5
SUCCESS

Discussion point
Students' own answers

Video
Before you watch
1 and 2
Students' own answers
3 *Possible answer: Silicon Valley* is in the state of California, in the U.S.A., and was once home to computer manufacturers, and now the world's largest high-tech companies are based there. *Hiring partner* is a synonym for employer, someone who hires you to do a job.

While you watch
1 F (He studied there two years ago.)
2 F (The course is ten weeks.)
3 T
4 T
5 T

After you watch
Students' own answers

Listening 1
A Vocabulary preview
1
1 e   2 h   3 f   4 g   5 a   6 c   7 d   8 b
2
1 situation
2 Though
3 surprised
4 effort
5 reward
6 admitted
7 load
8 apply

B Before you listen
Students' own answers

C Global listening
1 b   2 a

D Close listening
1
1 sense
2 pressure
3 subjects
4 skill
5 relieved
6 admission
2
Students' own answers

E Critical thinking
Students' own answers

Study skills
Students' own answers

Listening 2
A Vocabulary preview
1
1 According to
2 graduate
3 career
4 minimum
5 disagree
6 attempted
7 society

2
Students' own answers

B Before you listen
Students' own answers

C Global listening
1
b
2
2, 3, 5, 8, 9
3
3 B
Possible answer: It is direct and includes the main ideas, without extra details or examples.

D Close listening
1 F (Success is the achievement of something that you planned to do, or attempted to do.)
2 T
3 F (Bill Gates wanted to start a company.)
4 F (Anyone is successful if they're doing what they planned to do.)
5 T
6 F ("Beauty is in the eye of the beholder".)

E Critical thinking
Students' own answers

Pronunciation for listening
1
1 blew
2 night
3 do
4 seems
5 whether
2 and 3
Students' own answers

Vocabulary development
1
1 disappear—go away
2 inconsistent—not the same
3 dislike—not like
4 incomplete—not finished
5 impatient—not wanting to wait
6 rewrite—written again
7 overcautious—more careful than necessary
8 rearrange—put into a different order
2
1 disappear
2 dislike
3 incomplete
4 impatient
5 rearrange
6 rewrite
7 inconsistent
(Item 7 [overcautious] isn't used)
3
Students' own answers

Academic words
1 g   2 e   3 b   4 d   5 c   6 h   7 a   8 f
2
Students' own answers

Speaking model
Students' own answers

Grammar
1
1 significantly
2 most
3 A few
4 marginal
5 considerably
6 most
2
Possible answers
1 Most
2 a lot of
3 marginally
4 a little
5 considerably
6 a little

Speaking skill

1

Compare: as ... as, in the same way, like, likewise, similarly, the same as

Contrast: conversely, in contrast, on the contrary, unlike

2

1 However	4 unlike
2 In contrast	5 however
3 the same	6 Conversely

Pronunciation for speaking

1

1 staggering	4 As much as
2 remarkable	5 huge
3 Only	6 impressive

2

Students' own answers

Speaking task

Students' own answers

Review

Academic words review

1 illustrate	4 define
2 author	5 immigration
3 invest	

UNIT 6

PRESSURE

Discussion point

Students' own answers

Video

Before you watch

See While you watch 1

While you watch

1

1 15   2 20   3 500

2

1 Tokyo	3 men
2 choosing flowers in a shop	4 it relaxes them

After you watch

Students' own answers

Listening 1

A Vocabulary preview

1

1 h   2 b   3 c   4 a   5 e   6 g   7 f   8 d

2

1 support	5 logical
2 reasonable	6 exact
3 direct	7 call me
4 peer	8 left out

B Before you listen

1 4 5

C Global listening

1 b   2 f   3 a   4 e   5 g   6 c

(d is not mentioned)

D Close listening

1

1 S   2 S   3 L   4 L   5 S

2

1 d   2 a   3 c   4 e   5 b

E Critical thinking

Students' own answers

Pronunciation for listening

1

1 Takes time to think	4 Takes time to think
2 Doesn't take time to think	5 Doesn't take time to think
3 Takes time to think	6 Doesn't take time to think

2

1 Let's see. / I think peer pressure / is the pressure you get from your friends.

2 Um, / I think / most peer pressure situations / occur at school.

3 I think / it's after school.

4 So, / which is worse?

5 Um, / I suppose a teacher.

6 In my opinion, / no.

3

1 Um, let me think …	3 you know …
2 Well, …	4 uh, …

Listening 2

A Vocabulary preview

1

1 disappoint	5 outline
2 reduce	6 expectations
3 compete	7 distract
4 psychological	8 demands

2

Students' own answers

B Before you listen

Students' own answers

C Global listening

1, 3, 5, 6

D Close listening

1

1 being unprepared

2 high expectations from parents

3 competition from peers

4 other people in the exam room

5 the room and test-taking environment

6 when the test is scheduled

7 the test itself

2

1 anxious	5 depression
2 serious	6 may result in
3 as a result of	7 disappointment
4 physical	

E Critical thinking

Students' own answers

Study skills

1

1 c   2 f   3 b   4 e   5 a   6 d

2

Students' own answers

Vocabulary development

1

1 started	5 in touch
2 nowhere	6 behind someone
3 the message	7 going
4 good grades	8 in trouble

2

1 get in touch	5 get good grades
2 get started	6 get behind
3 get in trouble	7 get going
4 get the message	8 get nowhere

Academic words

1
1 g   2 f   3 e   4 a   5 d   6 h   7 c   8 b

2
1 depression
2 instance
3 psychology
4 revise
5 occur
6 specific
7 factor
8 sex

3
Students' own answers

Speaking model

A Analyze

1
1 d   2 a   3 b   4 c

2
Omar: cause—doesn't want to disappoint parents, effect—eats too much junk food, little exercise
Yuki: cause—doesn't have time to prepare for exams, effect—doesn't get good grades
Sara: cause—feels like she doesn't have enough money, effect—stays home all the time

B Discuss
Students' own answers

Grammar

1
1 If you don't understand the directions, you should ask the teacher.
2 If you feel anxious during an exam, you might try breathing deeply.
3 If you don't have enough time, you should answer the easy questions.
4 If you miss the exam, you could ask to take it later.
5 If you are well-prepared, you shouldn't have any problems.
6 If you don't have good test-taking skills, you might consider taking a class.

2
Students' own answers

Speaking skill

1
1 c   2 f   3 e   4 d   5 b   6 a

2
1 anxious
2 peer
3 in touch
4 direct
5 get going
6 compete

3
Students' own answers

Pronunciation for speaking

1
SHIRA: Anna, we can't go to the library today as it's closed.
ANNA: Oh no, I wanted to get some books. I have an exam Monday, and I really need to study. Do you know when it reopens?
SHIRA: I think it's open again tomorrow. You could try the library on the other side of town if you need the books today.
ANNA: Good idea! Do you want to come with me?
SHIRA: Yes, I'll be ready in an hour. I need to drop off some books. My exams finished yesterday.
ANNA: Oh wow, lucky you. I still have three more to take.

2
SHIRA: Anna, we can't go to the library today as it's closed.
ANNA: Oh no, I wanted to get some books. I have an exam Monday, and I really need to study. Do you know when it reopens?
SHIRA: I think it's open again tomorrow. You could try the library on the other side of town if you need the books today.
ANNA: Good idea! Do you want to come with me?
SHIRA: Yes, I'll be ready in an hour. I need to drop off some books. My exams finished yesterday.
ANNA: Oh wow, lucky you. I still have three more to do.

Speaking task
Students' own answers

Review

Academic words review
1 factor
2 revise
3 complement
4 specific
5 tense

UNIT 7
FEAR

Discussion point
Students' own answers

Video

Before you watch
1 c   2 a   3 b   4 d   5 e

While you watch
1 F (The slide is on the outside of a tall building.)
2 T
3 T
4 F (Only one person says she has a fear of heights.)
5 F (It is not well-known for its tall buildings.)

After you watch
Students' own answers

Listening 1

A Vocabulary preview

1
1 g   2 h   3 b   4 e   5 f   6 d   7 c   8 a

2
Students' own answers

B Before you listen
Students' own answers

C Global listening
1 c   2 e   3 b   4 g   5 d   6 a   7 f

D Close listening

1
1 Facts
2 fear
3 equally
4 Men
5 negative
6 Tips
7 time
8 memorize
9 main
10 stress
11 audience
12 Prepared

2
1 c   2 e   3 b   4 a   5 f   6 d

E Critical thinking
Students' own answers

Pronunciation for listening

1
1 you know
2 So, like,
3 I mean,
4 kind of
5 You see,
6 And, um,

2
1 A   2 B   3 B   4 A   5 B   6 B

3
1 It's OK to have fears.
2 Everyone is afraid of something.
3 Talk about your fears with a friend.
4 Don't let your fears affect your career.

Listening 2

A Vocabulary preview

1

1 b   2 h   3 f   4 a   5 c   6 d   7 g   8 e

2

1 frightened
2 powerless
3 certain
4 awful
5 control
6 seek
7 overcome
8 impair

B Before you listen

Students' own answers

C Global listening

elevators   public speaking   snakes   spiders   water

D Close listening

1

1 phobias
2 It helps keep us safe.
3 heart beats faster, hard to breathe, might get a sick feeling
4 elevators
5 Her new office was on the tenth floor.

2

✓ realizing she needed help
✓ techniques to help her relax
✓ deep breathing
✓ talking about what scared her
✓ watching the elevator
✓ standing in the elevator
✓ taking the elevator up only one floor
✓ taking the elevator up one floor at a time
✓ taking the elevator to the tenth floor

E Critical thinking

Students' own answers

Study skills

1

a 5   b 2   c 1   d 4   e 6   f 3

2

Students' own answers

Vocabulary development

1

careful / careless
harmful / harmless
helpful / helpless
pointless
powerful / powerless
truthful
wonderful
worthless

2

1 wonderful
2 fearful
3 harmful
4 stressful
5 successful
6 pointless
7 homeless

Academic words

1

1 c   2 f   3 a   4 e   5 h   6 b   7 g   8 d

2

1 technique
2 author
3 impact
4 definition
5 affect
6 survey
7 resource
8 automatic

3

Students' own answers

Speaking model

A Analyze

1

1 b   2 e   3 d   4 c   5 a

2

1 He summarizes what he is going to say.
2 He presents his problem.
3 He explains his problem in more detail.
4 He asks if the audience has any questions.

3

I have found, I have made, I have already made, I haven't met, I still haven't had
Something that happened in the past.

B Discuss

Students' own answers

Grammar

1

1 Sally has already given that speech three times.
2 Have you ever seen a 10-centimeter-long spider?
3 Jeff hasn't practiced his talk yet.
4 I still haven't spoken with a doctor about my fear of heights.
5 Have they taken their final exams yet?
6 They have never felt comfortable in small, closed spaces.

2

1 Samantha has already uploaded a video of her talk.
2 Glenn has not told anyone about his fear of flying yet.
3 Iris still has not shared her fears with her friends.
4 I have never met anyone with a fear of cats.

Speaking skill

1

1 any questions, feel free to ask
2 I'm sorry, but I don't have
3 I've already answered that

2

Students' own answers

Pronunciation for speaking

1, 2, and 3

First, she had to face her fears. After talking about her fears, ➡
and after learning to relax, she started to watch the elevator. In the beginning, she just watched people getting on, ⬅ getting off, smiling, and talking with others. ➡The next day, she watched it again. But then we stepped into the elevator, together. It didn't go anywhere—we just let the doors open and close automatically. She was nervous,➡ but by breathing deeply and relaxing, she was in control. ⬅ The next day, we repeated the first two steps, and then finally took the elevator up, but only one floor. We repeated this over several days, ⬅ adding one floor each day.

Speaking task

Students' own answers

Review

Academic words review

1 definition
2 survey
3 technique
4 resource
5 impact

UNIT 8

STORIES

Discussion point

Students' own answers

Video

Before you watch

Students' own answers

While you watch

1 wheel
2 safety gear
3 the weather
4 slippery

After you watch

Students' own answers

Listening 1

A Vocabulary preview

1

1 g   2 e   3 c   4 b   5 a   6 f   7 h   8 d

2

1 miss	5 afford
2 counter	6 obvious
3 visa	7 reserve
4 curious	8 system

3

Students' own answers

B Before you listen

Students' own answers

C Global listening

1

✓ how he got to the airport
✓ why he was late for the airport
✓ something he forgot to pack
✓ where he sat on the plane

2

b

D Close listening

1

1 e He bought a plane ticket to London.
2 a He got a visa.
3 b He made sure his flight was confirmed.
4 f He changed money.
5 d He called to book a taxi.
6 c He went home to get his passport.

2

1 missed	5 middle
2 woman	6 change
3 passport	7 first
4 waited	8 conference

E Critical thinking

Students' own answers

Study skills

Students' own answers

Listening 2

A Vocabulary preview

1

1 f   2 h   3 g   4 a   5 e   6 c   7 d   8 b

2

Students' own answers

B Before you listen

Students' own answers

C Global listening

1

Exposition	Falling Action
Rising Action	Resolution
Climax	

2

1 Exposition	4 Falling Action
2 Rising Action	5 Resolution
3 Climax	

D Close listening

1

Possible answers

Exposition: introduces characters and their relationships, the setting, the background story
Rising Action: plot thickens, main character faces a conflict, tension builds

Climax: high point, main event, moment of greatest danger / fear / emotion
Falling Action: character begins to deal with conflict
Resolution: conflict ends, questions are answered

2

1 five	5 effects
2 relationships between them	6 less
3 conflict	7 answered
4 exciting	

3 and 4

1 Exposition	4 Rising action
2 Climax	5 Falling action
3 Resolution	

E Critical thinking

Students' own answers

Pronunciation for listening

1 and 2

1 really	4 enormous
2 obviously	5 totally
3 extremely	6 huge

3

1 tiny	4 awful
2 totally	5 Obviously
3 long	6 extremely

4

Students' own answers

Vocabulary development

1

1 e   2 c   3 b   4 f   5 a   6 d

2

1 strange	4 amazing
2 plain	5 ugly
3 curious	6 loud

3

1 The service at our hotel was awful / horrible / terrible.
2 The lion's eyes were massive / enormous / huge.
3 A kind / friendly / helpful woman showed me how to find the mall.
4 The weather on our trip was excellent / pleasant / great.
5 The restaurant served tiny / little / baby-sized food portions.
6 We saw one lovely / attractive / beautiful sunset after another.

Academic words

1

1 d   2 f   3 c   4 b   5 a   6 g   7 h   8 e

2

1 accommodation	5 confirmed
2 fee	6 element
3 currency	7 drama
4 tension	8 analysis

3

Students' own answers

Speaking model

A Analyze

1

1 a few months ago	4 then
2 The week before	5 Finally
3 the next day	

2

No

B Discuss

Possible answers
I saw a boat in my yard instead!
I just laughed.
The delivery person just smiled.

Grammar
1
1 were climbing
2 was writing
3 were watching
4 was shining, were singing

2
1 were waiting, started
2 got, was sleeping
3 fell, was walking
4 were hurrying, had

3
Students' own answers

Speaking skill
1
1 b   2 c   3 a   4 e   5 f   6 d   7 i   8 g   9 h

2
1 Basically
2 Honestly
3 Thankfully
4 Clearly
5 Luckily

Pronunciation for speaking
1 and 2
1 bag
2 (C)alled, getting gas
3 (C)ounter
4 ba(ck), bag
5 boo(k), (C)ab

3
There was once a young boy who lived near a dar(k) forest. Every day he had to ta(k)e (C)are of his sheep. The young boy was lonely, and bored. He decided on a plan to relieve his boredom. He ran into the village shouting, "Wolf! Wolf!" People (C)ame to help but there was no wolf. This amused the boy, so he did it again. Again, there was no wolf, so the people wal(k)ed away.
Soon after that, a wolf really did (C)ome into the village, and began eyeing his sheep. He was extremely frightened. He (C)ried, "Wolf! Help! This time, there really is a wolf!" The wolf (C)ame (C)loser and (C)loser to his sheep.

Speaking task
Students' own answers

Review
Academic words review
1 currency
2 analysis
3 fee
4 recover
5 tension

UNIT 9 >
ENVIRONMENT

Discussion point
Students' own answers

Video
Before you watch
1 d   2 c   3 e   4 b   5 a

While you watch
1 F (The Solarbox is green.)
2 T
3 F (Two university graduates from the London School of Economics invented it.)
4 T
5 T

After you watch
Students' own answers

Listening 1
A Vocabulary preview
1
1 f   2 e   3 g   4 b   5 a   6 d   7 h   8 c

2
1 fuel
2 dishwasher
3 solar, store
4 supply, renewable
5 install, panels

3
Students' own answers

B Before you listen
Students' own answers

C Global listening
1 a   2 a   3 b   4 c

D Close listening
Pros:
2 batteries
4 clean
5 sell
6 cheaper
7 quiet
Cons:
2 expensive
4 building
5 high
6 space

E Critical thinking
Students' own answers

Study skills
Students' own answers

Listening 2
A Vocabulary preview
1
1 f   2 e   3 a   4 h   5 d   6 g   7 b   8 c

2
Students' own answers

B Before you listen
Students' own answers

C Global listening
1
1 the title (Eco-tourism)
2 the definition (Eco-tourism is …)
3 the aims (It aims …)
4 the pros (The good)
5 the animal picture
6 the cons (The bad)
7 the dancers picture
8 the snorkeling picture
9 the tips

2
c

D Close listening
1
1 She invites someone to listen.
2 She further explains an idea.
3 She refers to a visual.
4 She offers additional information.

2
1 a   2 d   3 e   4 c   5 f   6 b

E Critical thinking
Students' own answers

Pronunciation for listening
1
1 /j/
2 /w/
3 /j/
4 /w/
5 /j/
6 /j/
7 /w/
8 /w/

2
1 you a /w/
2 money or /j/
3 allow us /w/
4 who are /w/
5 go on /w/
6 see if /j/

Vocabulary development

1
1 attract – attraction
2 conserve—conservation
3 damage—damage
4 develop—development
5 install—installation
6 question—question
7 pollute—pollution
8 power—power
9 preserve —preservation
10 produce—production
11 supply—supply

2
1 pollution
2 argument
3 power
4 conserve
5 attract
6 develop / produce
7 damage

3
Students' own answers

Academic words

1
1 d   2 c   3 e   4 a   5 f   6 h   7 b   8 g

2
1 definite
2 potential
3 relevant
4 capacity
5 fees
6 convert
7 guarantee
8 data

3
Students' own answers

Speaking model

A Analyze

1
1 Would you like to hear about wind power
2 As you see here on this poster
3 Notice in this picture that
4 Let me just add that
5 I'm happy to send you a link

2
First, Second, Finally, Also, Another

B Discuss
Students' own answers

Grammar

1
1 be finished
2 be found
3 be taught
4 be sold
5 be saved
6 be replaced

2
1 The rules in the national park have to be followed.
2 Great eco-tourism deals can be found online.
3 Computers should be put to sleep at night.
4 The eco-tour can't be paid for with a credit card.

3
Students' own answers

Speaking skill

1
1 That's interesting.
2 I like that idea.
3 Can you tell me more about that?
4 What does that graph represent?
5 Can you talk a little more about that?
6 Excuse me. Can I ask a quick question?
7 Sorry, but can I ask a question?
8 What do you mean by that?

2
1 Sounds great.
2 Can you talk a little more about that?
3 Sorry, but can I ask a question?
4 What do you mean by that?

3 and 4
Students' own answers

Pronunciation for speaking

1
1 be<u>ne</u>fit
2 in<u>stall</u>
3 pre<u>serve</u>
4 el<u>ec</u>tric
5 pre<u>sent</u>
6 in<u>form</u>
7 pre<u>pare</u>
8 en<u>vir</u>onment

2 and 3
1 bene<u>fi</u>cial
2 instal<u>la</u>tion
3 preser<u>va</u>tion
4 el<u>ec</u>trical
5 presen<u>ta</u>tion
6 infor<u>ma</u>tion
7 prepa<u>ra</u>tion
8 environ<u>men</u>tally

Speaking task
Students' own answers

Review

Academic words review
1 potential
2 convert
3 data
4 capacity
5 affect

UNIT 10 ⟩
MEDICINE

Discussion point
Students' own answers

Video

Before you watch
1 e   2 b   3 a   4 d   5 c

While you watch
1 a   2 b   3 a

After you watch
Students' own answers

Listening 1
A Vocabulary preview

1
1 e   2 a   3 g   4 b   5 c   6 f   7 h   8 d

2
1 prescription
2 upload
3 concern
4 persuade
5 abuse
6 matter
7 convenient
8 rely on

3
Students' own answers

B Before you listen
Students' own answers

C Global listening

1
1 accuracy of doctor's assessment
2 convenience of getting medical care
3 giving a prescription for medicine
4 access to medical care
5 how personal the experience is
6 getting a second opinion from another doctor
7 patient privacy
8 abuse of the healthcare system
9 cost of medical care
Not discussed: dependence on technology

2 and 3
Students' own answers

D Close listening
1 CS   2 CS   3 FS   4 EO   5 EO   6 ED

E Critical thinking
Students' own answers

Study skills
1
1 b   2 c   3 a

2
1 To persuade the reader that natural treatments are not always better.
2 Modern medicine is better than natural treatments.
3 To accept the scientific evidence for modern medicine's effectiveness.
4 Diseases such as polio, and small pox have been cured by modern medicine.

Listening 2
A Vocabulary preview
1 a   2 e   3 h   4 d   5 g   6 b   7 c   8 f

2
Students' own answers

B Before you listen
Students' own answers

C Global listening
1 Countries   3 Key Statistics   5 Benefits
2 The Top Five   4 The Process   6 Drawbacks

D Close listening
1 F (He thinks it's more of a marketing term.)
2 T
3 F (He says that, understandably, the patient expects some sort of money to be paid back.)
4 T

E Critical thinking
Students' own answers

Pronunciation for listening
1 and 2
1 But let's see if it works.
2 I'll begin now by answering that question.
3 As you can see, it is not tourism exactly.
4 It's simply getting treatment in another country.
5 The amount the patient saves will depend on the country, and the treatment type.
6 In these cases, the patient understandably expects some sort of money to be paid back.

3
1 help prevent   3 make cosmetic   5 manage just
2 if follow-up   4 job before

Vocabulary development
1
1 e   2 d   3 a   4 b   5 c   6 h   7 i   8 f   9 g   10 j

2
1 clinic, hospice, nursing home
2 cure, pill
3 home health aid, surgeon, therapist
4 disease, flu
Possible additional answers:
Places to receive care: hospital, health center
Things that help / make us feel good: medicine, treatments
People who give care: doctor, nurse
Things that harm / make us feel bad: a cold, a virus

3
Students' own answers

Academic words
1
1 a   2 c   3 b   4 b   5 c   6 b   7 b

2
Students' own answers

Speaking model
A Analyze
1 and 2
saying the other side's argument is not true or accurate:
I don't think that's really true.
I'm afraid that's not accurate.
two questions that are asked:
Do you know what percentage of people are happy to see online doctors?
Can you tell me what a second opinion is?
The questions are indirect in that they begin with Do you know / Can you tell me + a statement

B Discuss
Students' own answers

Grammar
1
1 Can you tell me what a good country for eye care is?
2 Do you know if my medical insurance covers hospice care?
3 (Do you know) when medical tourism first became popular?
4 (Do you remember) if your second opinion was the same as your first opinion?

2
1 Do you know what the phone number of the hospital is?
2 Can you tell me if your doctor takes this type of insurance?
3 Do you have an idea how much the hospice charges each day?
4 Can you tell us when tomorrow's debate will begin?

3
Students' own answers

Speaking skill
1 and 2
1 b   2 d   3 e   4 c   5 a

3
Students' own answers

Pronunciation for speaking
1
1 can—emphatic   4 no—citation
2 no—contrastive   5 more—contrastive
3 big—emphatic

2
A: really (emphatic), B: p.m. (citation), evening (emphatic),
B: only (contrastive), A: twice (emphatic), B: two (contrastive),
B: medical (contrastive), eye (contrastive)

Speaking task
Students' own answers

Review
Academic words review
1 procedure   4 medical
2 guarantee   5 residents
3 vision

Academic words revision
Units 1–5
1 author   5 abstract   9 strategy
2 participate   6 illustrate   10 furthermore
3 paragraph   7 eventually
4 evidence   8 define

Units 6–10
1 techniques   5 factor   9 automatic
2 survey   6 data   10 vision
3 relevant   7 specific
4 revise   8 analysis

MARKING KEY FOR ASSESSMENT CRITERIA >>

25 points: Excellent achievement. Student successfully fulfills the expectation for this part of the assignment with little or no room for improvement.

20 points: Good achievement. Student fulfills the expectation for this part of the assignment, but may have a few errors or need some improvement.

15 points: Satisfactory achievement. Student needs some work to fulfill the expectation for this part of the assignment, but shows some effort.

5 points: Poor achievement. Student does not fulfill the expectation for this part of the assignment.

UNIT 1 SOCIETY >

Student name: _____

Date: _____

Unit assignment: Discuss a charity to donate to

	25 points	20 points	15 points	5 points
The student uses discourse markers for adding reasons or details successfully.				
The student gives reasons or explanations for their opinion.				
The student uses weak forms and the schwa sound correctly.				

Total: _____ / 75

Comments:

- -

UNIT 2 FOOD >

Student name: _____

Date: _____

Unit assignment: Present advice on reducing food waste

	25 points	20 points	15 points	5 points
The student uses relative clauses correctly.				
The student offers appropriate advice and suggestions.				
The student pronounces words with consonant clusters clearly and correctly.				

Total: _____ / 75

Comments:

Skillful Second Edition Level 2 Listening & Speaking Teacher's Book.
This page is photocopiable, but all copies must be complete pages.
© Macmillan Publishers Limited 2018.

UNIT 3 BUSINESS

Student name: _____

Date: _____

Unit assignment: Present a business plan

	25 points	20 points	15 points	5 points
The student uses modal verbs for advice accurately.				
The student takes turns in conversation appropriately.				
The student chunks their presentation effectively.				

Total: _____ / 75

Comments:

UNIT 4 TRENDS

Student name: _____

Date: _____

Unit assignment: Describe a timeline of a city

	25 points	20 points	15 points	5 points
The student uses the simple past to order events chronologically.				
The student asks for clarification and repetition clearly and concisely.				
The student places stress in phrases connected with *and* correctly.				

Total: _____ / 75

Comments:

UNIT 5 SUCCESS

Student name: _____

Date: _____

Unit assignment: Present data on what influences exam success

	25 points	20 points	15 points	5 points
The student uses quantifiers to describe numbers appropriately.				
The student uses discourse markers to compare and contrast effectively.				
The student uses stress in modifiers before data accurately.				

Total: _____ / 75

Comments:

UNIT 6 PRESSURE

Student name: _____

Date: _____

Unit assignment: Discuss ways to reduce pressure on students

	25 points	20 points	15 points	5 points
The student gives advice using modals in conditional sentences effectively.				
The student explains something they don't know the word for clearly.				
The student pronounces consonant sounds at word boundaries accurately.				

Total: _____ / 75

Comments:

UNIT 7 FEAR

Student name: _____

Date: _____

Unit assignment: Give a presentation on a problem you had to solve

	25 points	20 points	15 points	5 points
The student uses the present perfect tense with adverbs effectively.				
The student invites and responds to questions appropriately.				
The student uses pausing and pacing when speaking confidently.				

Total: _____ / 75

Comments:

UNIT 8 STORIES

Student name: _____

Date: _____

Unit assignment: Prepare and tell a story

	25 points	20 points	15 points	5 points
The student uses the past progressive accurately.				
The student uses sentence adverbs correctly.				
The student pronounces the sounds /g/ and /k/ successfully.				

Total: _____ / 75

Comments:

UNIT 9 ENVIRONMENT

Student name: _____

Date: _____

Unit assignment: Present a poster on the environment

	25 points	20 points	15 points	5 points
The student uses modal passives accurately.				
The student listens to and interacts with other presenters appropriately.				
The student uses stress in word suffixes correctly.				

Total: _____ / 75

Comments:

UNIT 10 MEDICINE

Student name: _____

Date: _____

Unit assignment: Take part in a debate about patient care

	25 points	20 points	15 points	5 points
The student uses indirect questions correctly.				
The student refutes arguments effectively.				
The student uses citation, contrastive, and/or emphatic stress appropriately.				

Total: _____ / 75

Comments:

Skillful Second Edition Level 2 Listening & Speaking Teacher's Book.
This page is photocopiable, but all copies must be complete pages.
© Macmillan Publishers Limited 2018.